ABOVE
THE
CRY
OF
BATTLE

To: Abi —
a friend and partner
for Christ & His Kingdom

Chuck Holsinger
Prov. 3:5,6

ABOVE
THE
CRY
OF
BATTLE

CHUCK HOLSINGER

ACW Press
Phoenix, Arizona 85013

Above the Cry of Battle
Copyright ©2001 Chuck Holsinger
All rights reserved

Cover Design by
Interior design by Pine Hill Graphics

Packaged by ACW Press
5501 N. 7th Ave., #502
Phoenix, Arizona 85013
www.acwpress.com
The views expressed or implied in this work do not necessarily reflect those of ACW Press. Ultimate design, content, and editorial accuracy of this work is the responsibility of the author(s).

Publisher's Cataloging-in-Publication Data
(Provided by Quality Books, Inc.)

Holsinger, Chuck
 Above the cry of battle / Chuck Holsinger. -- 1st ed.

  p. cm.
  ISBN 1-892525-55-0

  1. Holsinger, Chuck. 2. World War, 1939-1945--
Campaigns--Philippines. 3. World War, 1939-1945--
Personal narratives, American. 4. Soldiers--United
States--Biography. 5. War--Moral and ethical aspects.
I. Title.

  D767.4.H65 2001   940.54'25'092
                               QBI01-700691

Printed in the United States of America.

DEDICATED

To those living today who enabled me to survive the war and its trauma. There are four specific persons who are in this roll of honor: first, my little sister Laura, who wrote to me faithfully every week; second, my oldest brother "Hap" who mentored and encouraged me to memorize Bible verses; third, a soldier-buddy from the Thirty-fifth Infantry, Dick Lawrenz, who is a Christian and a special friend; and fourth but not least, Betty, my wife and partner for fifty years, whom I did not meet until after the war, but who has been understanding, sympathetic, and a source of strength, as I relived the war over and over again.

CONTENTS

Foreword 9

Acknowledgments 13

Introduction. 17

Prologue 25

1. Excitement on Board—Land in Sight 33

2. Liberation—Bitter and Sweet 39

3. Harsh Reality—We're at War. 45

4. "Dalton's Army". 51

5. Lupao Town—First Battle 57

6. The Bible Is for Real! 75

7. Intimate Talks with God 81

8. Enemy of a Different Kind. 87

9. Capintalan Ridge and Maggot Hill 93

10. Another Ridge, Another Deliverance. 101

11. Example of Filipino Courage. 105

12. Every Choice a Crisis 111

13. Moran, Short-term Partner 117

14. The War Behind Me. 125

15. Challenge—Return to the Battle Scene 127

16. Excitement in Ministry 133

17. Revisiting War Areas 139

18. Recalling God's Goodness at Digdig 147

19. Remembering Miracles Along Highway 5 153

20. Another Japanese Invasion? 171

21. Divine Detour 177

22. Unforgettable Mike 183

23. I Meet Yukiko 187

24. Honor Beyond Expectation 193

25. Appreciation Beyond Words 199

26. Unexpected Surprise 201

27. Stunning Turnabout 205

28. Japanese Missionary in the Philippines 208

   Epilogue 223
   Notes 227
   Glossary 229
   Components of an Army 230
   Tour of Duty 231
   Appendix 233

FOREWORD

Private First Class Charles D. Holsinger, an infantry scout in the 25th Infantry Division, was awarded the Silver Star for gallantry in action on 28 February 1945 at Maringalo, Luzon, Philippine Islands. In a night attack, Japanese forces killed, wounded, and forced withdrawal of a six-man outpost until only PFC Holsinger was left. Outnumbered, he refused to retreat and fought Japanese soldiers at close range until reinforced by other members of his platoon.

This was not gee-whiz technological warfare from a stand-off position fifteen thousand feet above the enemy. This was close combat at the most raw elemental level—blood, bayonets and bodies torn apart, burned or decayed. This is a book by someone who has "been there." Holsinger's words have the ring of authenticity to them. Combat veterans will attest to the realities spoken of, written not for shock effect, but simply to tell what happened. For those who may wonder what ground combat is like, there will be a necessary revulsion. But if human degradation is depicted starkly, so also is human nobility lifted up.

Dietrich Bonhoeffer spoke of "the view from below." In World War II, there was no one below the infantry ground soldier, the draftee or enlistee who crawled on his belly and whose life depended on digging foxholes in the ground. But like a golden thread running through this book, this is the U.S. citizen army at its best, ordinary Americans demonstrating extraordinary resourcefulness, camaraderie, bravery and yes, heroism.

No one will be able to read these pages without being impressed by the uncommon selflessness and caring of these GIs. But more, this book is a tribute to the courage and sacrifice of Filipinos who gratefully risked their lives for their country in solidarity with Americans.

But where is the Divine Presence in all of this? That is the question I asked as an infantryman in the Korean War, when my best friend was killed five hundred yards from my position by Chinese artillery fire. He was the most beautiful human being I have ever known and the most committed Christian I ever met, and yet he was not spared. I am still processing this. However, this does not prevent me from saying that amidst all the chaos and carnage Charles experienced, I have no doubt whatsoever that God worked in a providential and miraculous way in and through his life. When a fellow GI commented, "You are more like a cat with nine lives than a human!" it was a secular way of saying that something awfully mysterious was going on in the life of Charles Holsinger. Early Christians were called "witnesses" or "martyrs," those who witnessed to their faith, even unto death. Charles' witness to his personal faith in Jesus Christ consisted not only of repeated encounters with death, but in miraculous escapes from it.

At the very deepest level, this book is about another war, the war within. Deep within Charles Holsinger was a consuming hatred for the Japanese, which was at war with the love he knew in Jesus Christ. Perhaps the greatest miracle of all recorded in this book is the change that took place in Charles' life, enabling him to forgive the Japanese people. When Jesus performed bodily miracles, people expressed amazement when He also claimed the authority to forgive sin. In 165 consecutive days of combat, Charles' life was miraculously spared. He was equally startled and surprised when God reached into his life, allowing him to forgive. But this was no instantaneous miracle. This was a painful struggle—inner combat—which went on for some time. The miracle is that God met Charles in the struggle. God graciously entered Charles' inner battle in both quiet and jarring ways to perform a healing. This book is about Staff Sergeant Charles Holsinger, a liberation soldier. But it is also about a liberated soldier.

KERMIT D. JOHNSON
Chaplain (Major General), USA (Ret.)

———————————

This book is about a man of missions—one who is every inch a hero both in the battlefield and missions field. He is a hero because he is a man very much in touch with himself: with his fears, as well as with his passion to conquer the enemy, as he must. But in the process he sees within himself a bigger and a fiercer enemy lurking. This then opens up a new battleground requiring a new set of weaponry. The fury of the battle within matches the demands of the mission field outside.

The book also depicts battle scenes of World War II on Philippine soil. The strategy and tactics of battle are woven together with battle maps, sketches and snapshots. A natural storyteller, Sgt. Chuck Holsinger writes with vividness and simplicity.

The Great Commission Missionary Training Center (GCMTC) takes pride in publishing *Above the Cry of Battle*, for its maiden publishing venture.

MET CASTILLO, President-Founder
REY O. HALILI, Chair of the Board
Great Commission Missionary Training Center

ACKNOWLEDGMENTS

This book has been a team effort. There is no way that I could have written this book without the help of others. I am sure that some of you will wonder how I remember so many details. I am especially indebted to a fellow soldier—a man I never met—who has kept me on track with the sequence of events. He is William "Bill" de Jarnette Rutherfoord. Bill got permission from his commanding officer to draw ink sketches of the Luzon Campaign, and the artwork in this book is his record of the men—I being one of them—who battled for every inch of Philippine soil.

In September, 1945, Bill penned the following introduction to his 176 sketches:

"My desire to do this [sketching] came from the fact that I have seen reproductions of a large number of 'war pictures' which were done by competent artists, but which lacked an intimate understanding of their principal subject, 'G.I. Joe.' To paint life, one must understand it, and to understand it, one must 'live.' Therefore, by the same token, I say, to paint a soldier, one must *be* a soldier.

"I have dug latrines [make-shift toilets] and cleaned them, pulled K.P [kitchen duty], and helped build roads through bottomless jungle. I have 'policed up' cigarette butts, beer bottles, and leaves all the way across the Pacific, and got drunk in pubs. I have been enraged by the high-handed arrogance of some of our officers and inspired by the unassuming excellence of others. At times, I have wished I were dead, only to snap out of it a little later and be intoxicated by the joy of living. I have spent years at the old Army games of 'hurry up and wait,' and 'move it over there, then, move it back again,' while small boys called me 'Joe." In other words, I am a 'G.I.,' and this is how the Luzon Campaign looked to me.

"Many of my sketches were actually done under fire, while some had to be done from memory, because of such things as rain, darkness, and the violence of sudden, unexpected action. I hate a lie, and, therefore, if anything of importance has been left out of my story [sketches], it is because I did not see it."

In late fall 1945 I received a letter from Headquarters, 25th Infantry Division. It stated in part that for $4.00 I could obtain a pictorial remembrance of our campaign on Luzon. I responded and shortly thereafter received Bill Rutherfoord's sketches. They have been my treasure to this day.

In 1992, when I started to write this book, I began a search for Bill Rutherfoord so I could get his permission to use his sketches. After no success in locating him, I thought he might have passed away. I finished my book, and it was published in the Philippines. But I knew that there could be no U.S. edition without Rutherfoord's permission.

Earlier this year, by way of a friend's computer and a few phone calls, I finally found Bill Rutherfoord. It was February 28, 2001, and I learned that he was suffering from cancer and that his life expectancy was short. The miracle is that although he was weak, he was lucid.

Bill and I, along with his wife June, had a warm and friendly conversation, and, in that time on the phone, it was like

Bill and I had known each other forever. Bill was more than happy to give me permission to reprint his artwork. On March 7, he signed the authorization. Three days later Bishop Rutherfoord of the Anglican Catholic Church went to his eternal home.

In this whole relationship I have sensed a divine purpose. Because of Bill's sketches and my writing, I believe that we have been able to capture both the reality of war as well as God's hand in the midst of this great conflict. It is a miracle that our lives finally crossed. I can say similarly regarding Bill's faith and the testimony of Holy Scripture regarding Abel's faith (Hebrews 11:4): "by faith Bill still speaks, even though he is dead." This is my confidence and this is my hope.

As I looked on the task of writing this book, I didn't think I could do it. To relive all of the emotions of the war seemed like a mountain too high to scale. But in the midst of this ambivalence, there were three people who committed themselves to me to get the book finished.

Lloyd Cory also endured the war. We were called to active duty together. Then we traveled by troop ship, USS Sea Witch, across the vast Pacific. We endured looking at the endless sea for twenty-three days, finally arriving at the island of New Caledonia and the 5th Replacement Depot. Out paths then parted: He went to the 43rd Division while my assignment was the 25th Division. He knows and understands a soldier's life, and he agreed to help me "cross the finish line." Lloyd is a successful author in his own right, and his experience with the printed page has been invaluable.

Mrs. Lois Vogen has been a partner in every sense of the word, having served together in the same inter-church overseas mission agency, OC International, for seventeen years. In a chance meeting, she asked how I was getting along with my book and offered her assistance. This offer was like a gift from heaven, and her computer skills and knowledge of grammar greatly facilitated the project.

My "compatriot" Paul Yaggy served in the Navy during World War II. He also served our country for many years as Director, Research, Development and Engineering, US Army Aviation Systems Command (as a research scientist in aerodynamics). He retired early and became a significant member of the president's team for OC International. Following his distinguished career with the U.S. government, like Bill Rutherfoord and myself he ended up in service for God's kingdom. He has been as close as a blood brother. Together, we have spent hours to make sure that details of the book are right.

INTRODUCTION

During World War II and for years thereafter, I came to the conclusion that there was no reason to forgive the Japanese—their treachery was too great, their evil too gross, the pain they inflicted too deep, the casualties too many, and the wounds too severe. And after all, they started the war with their heinous attack on Pearl Harbor, and we finished it! In my own heart I felt that they were beyond forgiveness.

This was one soldier who hated the Japanese. I took as my motto, "The only good Japanese is a dead one." There was a certain glee in standing over a dead Japanese. I am not proud of this but it was reality.

I remember vividly the rush of excitement of my first experience. Early on in the campaign for Luzon Island, our ten-man patrol was moving across no-man's-land, seeking the enemy and checking out suspicious areas. We had been attacked the night before, so emotions and tension were high. As we started out that morning, we were certain that the enemy wasn't too far away.

Jack and I were scouts—first men out—moving slowly down a dusty road about a hundred yards ahead of the rest of the unit. Shortly into our assignment, Jack reached a little bridge, and was cautiously checking it out for signs of dynamite or booby traps. (The Japanese were famous for doing such things.) I was about twenty yards behind him, kneeling on the road with my rifle ready and prepared to give him cover if anything happened.

As he moved toward the edge of the bridge, he suddenly went flat on his stomach, and then began pulling back. He rolled on his side, and waved me forward. He had seen something suspicious. Sure enough, there were some papers and trash with Japanese printing in the dry streambed.

We moved quietly to the other side and looked down. There were two feet in Japanese shoes! We moved back, and whispered a hasty decision. Jack took out a grenade, while I quickly moved to the opposite side. He pulled the pin and threw the grenade under the bridge. As the blast shattered the morning silence and filled the air with dust, we jumped down from both sides with rifles ready.

We found a dead Japanese soldier. The lieutenant and the others joined us in seconds. After carefully examining the enemy's blood-soaked uniform, it was determined he had been bleeding for several hours, and the grenade had simply ended his misery.

The exciting thing for both Jack and me was that we had a trophy! He was an army officer, and by the insignia on his uniform he was a captain. He had a German-made Luger pistol in his belt, and a three-foot-long *samurai* sword!

Now the "joy of the spoils of war" was ours. Since Jack was the first out, he had the pick of what we found. Jack took the pistol, and tucked it into his belt, and claimed the sword—real treasures of war. I searched the pockets and found a watch and a Japanese flag, signed by family and friends, wishing him "good luck." Almost every enemy soldier carried a flag like this one, either in a pocket or wrapped around his waist. This was one of the most prized possessions that an American soldier could call his own. It was mine. It had some blood on it, but that was OK. I could rinse it off later.

I kicked and rolled the body over with my foot, and found in the pocket over his heart a picture of a beautiful Japanese woman. I hesitated whether to take it or not. I decided to take it. Later that picture would play a significant role in my attitude toward the enemy, but for now it was simply a souvenir.

As I was leaving I looked down at the glassy eyes and sallow face, and I smiled, and said to myself, *Now there's a good Japanese!*

But I was wrong. It took years to correct my thinking and attitude, and I am thankful for God's patience. God led me step by step from the wounds of hate, anger, and resentment to forgiveness and healing. Along the way He provided miracles. The backdrop for most of this was the Philippines.

Originally it was my thought to leave an account of my experiences for my children and grandchildren. But I didn't want to just string together a series of war adventures. There were lessons learned that needed to be shared. Above everything else I wanted to give testimony to the reality of God and His faithfulness during the battles in the Philippines, and the subsequent impact of those events on my life. Intertwined with all of this has been my struggle to forgive, which I trust will be an encouragement to others.

The motivation to write this book came in 1992, when I was serving a second term as a missionary in the Philippines. I was having lunch with a special friend, Rey Halili, a successful Filipino businessman and publisher, whom I look up to and respect very much. The subject of World War II came up, and he asked if I would share some of my experiences. This I did. When lunch was over, he suggested that I get these stories down on paper.

Two weeks later Rey called and urged me to write about the fighting, my personal experiences, and the camaraderie between Filipinos and Americans. He felt that the latter should be preserved, and that his people needed to be reminded of this bond. He said that as the years have gone by, the friendly spirit between Filipinos and Americans has been eroding. The oneness between our people should not be lost. Then he added, "We need to give my people a historical memory because it's this that will keep the bond between Filipinos and Americans alive."

As I reflected on the subject, I was reminded time and time again of the GIs and Filipinos from World War II and the veterans from the Korean and the Vietnam Wars, who will not talk about their experiences. They have locked them up forever in their minds and hearts. This action has turned many of them into bitter and angry men and women. But I have found that in talking with them, they will open up when they learn that I was a frontline soldier. They know I understand, and for some it is the beginning of healing.

There is a tragedy in the lives of many soldiers and civilians who have endured traumá. Basically it is the unwillingness to bring personal issues out into the open, confess them, and move on with their lives. This is true of Americans as well as Filipinos. This lack of forgiveness has ruined individuals and families. I have a dear friend who told me that her father was a U.S. fighter pilot in the Pacific during World War II. He would never talk about his experiences. His only expressions were outbursts against the Japanese who had taken four years out of his life! He was so angry at them that he took it out on his family. He ended up making life miserable for everyone.

I learned early on that it is important to talk about the war. I had kept everything to myself thinking that no one would understand. However, getting these things out into the open brings a sense of "cleansing" in my heart and a positive response from others.

It has not been easy to write what is to follow. For us soldiers the war is never over, even though the rifles and cannons have been laid to rest. Its influence will be with us as long as we live. This means that there is pain and anxiety when the memories of the war are brought to the surface of our thinking. Many times I stopped writing, and told myself that it was not worth continuing.

On more than one occasion, I found myself so emotionally involved that I couldn't go on. At another time I was crying uncontrollably. I realized that I was grieving over thirty-two personal friends who were killed in my company after making the landing on the beach at Lingayen Gulf years ago. (There were other men, replacements, who joined us and died. Many of these I never even knew. Some died within days of joining our company.) When soldiers on the front line die, there is no time to grieve. It is too dangerous to think about the dead—protecting life is the priority.

No one seems to care about the dead. The fallen are wrapped in body bags, and hauled away. And the soldiers move on to their next objective. One of the benefits of this writing is that my grieving has come to pass—more than fifty years after the fact!

Some of this narrative had been shared verbally, but some had been held back. As years passed, I even began to deny some of my own experiences. This made me almost think that what I went through was simply a figment of my imagination. Did I really kill? Surely that was just a dream. No, it was and is reality. But I never killed people—I just killed the enemy! (What a terrible perspective on the value of human life!)

Perhaps the most important message to get across is that one cannot have a healthy life without forgiveness. Pain and suffering must be talked about, and faced. The ugliness of war and any other bad incident can leave either ugly scars or beauty marks. The choice is up to us. I chose to turn my scars into beauty marks.

But there is another reason for writing. While still a young man I made the decision to make God a part of my life— whether I lived or died. For some reason or another God spared my life. Some of my closest friends—even Christian buddies— died in the battlefields of the Southwest Pacific. On more than one occasion I have had to ask: "Lord, why them and not me?"

The Lord has a path for each one of us to walk. My path has been very clear, serving the Lord as a missionary since 1953. I am alive today because of His mercy and goodness. I do not see myself favored because I came through the war without a scratch. Rather I recognize a responsibility to make sure that I be and do (to the best of my ability) what I know God called me to be and to do. One of the things I should do is to write this account.

It is my prayer that this book will speak to many Filipinos and Americans. As you read, I trust you will find hope, mercy, and forgiveness. For this soldier it has been a long journey, but not without its rewards. I am reminded of the Bible verse, "Let us not become weary in doing good, for at the proper time we will reap a harvest if we do not give up." (Galatians 6:9).

In Proverbs 3:5 and 6 it states: "Trust in the Lord with all your heart and lean not on your own understanding; in all your ways acknowledge him, and he will make your paths straight." These verses have served to guide me. In war and peace they are my comfort and hope, especially when I am frustrated and when things are dark. There had been times in my life when I thought I was making the best choice only to learn later that my choice would have ended in disaster. Leaving things and circumstances in God's hands was a significant battlefield lesson that has carried over into my life and missionary experience.

My missionary career has intertwined with the Philippines and its people. After the war, my wife and I lived in the Philippines for a total of seven years. And when I was based in the United States, I returned to the Orient over seventy-nine times. At least forty of those trips took me to the Philippines to minister and take care of missions business.

Every trip back to the Philippines has been an enriching experience. However, lingering memories of the war would often make it difficult for me to return. Each visit brings back vivid dreams of battle. At the same time there is something that draws me back like a magnet. It's the Filipino people, who will always have a significant place in my heart.

The story that I am sharing is true. In some accounts I have purposely used fictitious names to protect the memory of those who have died. When I write about the Japanese army plans, it is what I remembered reading and hearing from intelligence reports. I have no reason to question the authenticity of the information that was shared with us, which was usually posted on the company bulletin board, or passed along to the troops as general information.

Some have said, "You have an amazing memory." I am grateful to one other man, whom I have never met, but who has kept me on track with the sequence of events. He is William de Jarnette Rutherfoord (see acknowledgment section). I have his pictorial record—copies of all 176 plates—to jog my memory. I also have a military map with arrows and dates that show the movement of our division along the path to our major objective of Balete Pass. Above everything else, the scenes of the war have been branded on my mind forever.

PROLOGUE

I n reflecting back on the war, a recurring question comes to mind: *Was the war worth the cost?*

As I look at our flags—"Old Glory" of the United States and the colors of the Republic of the Philippines—standing side by side, it gives me an emotional rush of excitement and pride. The red, white, and blue of America blends so well with the red, white, blue, and brilliant gold of the Philippine flag. I salute them with the greatest respect. Both are waving in the breeze signifying independence and freedom. *Freedom* and *Independence.* These two words say it all.

"YES! It was worth it!"

The Memorial Chapel, which is the focal point of the Manila American Cemetery, is flanked by these two flags that stand like guardian angels over the names and graves of those who gave their lives. As these emblems fly in the breeze, they silently say by their majestic presence, "It was worth it all!"

To this day whenever I see the Stars and Stripes pass by, I stand with a lump in my throat and tears in my eyes, as I think of all that it stands for. It was not that way until early on in the campaign when I first really saw it—the flag of my country!

We were returning from an all-day patrol. It had been horrible. Stinging insects were impossible to swat away. We forded a leech-infested stream through waist-deep water. Then we had to hike through a torrential downpour. This turned the dusty road into oozing mud, which clung to our boots and added pounds to each step. By early afternoon we still had a long way to go before returning to the safety of our perimeter. Exhaustion from the emotional stress of anticipating the enemy and physical exertion was taking over. I was almost at the place of despair, even saying to myself, *What's the use? I can't go on.*

As we staggered over the crest of a hill there it was in the distance—"Old Glory"! Someone had climbed a tree and hung up a U.S. flag! We all cheered, and I cried—there were goose pimples on my arms. Seeing the flag recharged us! There was new strength and hope. Before long we were all singing "America the Beautiful." Our steps quickened, and I said to myself, *Chuck, keep going, keep fighting and don't give up! Remember what is waiting for you at home!* The sight of our flag, waving in welcome, is forever etched in my mind. To this day I cannot close my eyes and focus on the mental image of the flag without tears. And in those moments I pray, *God, may it yet wave o'er the land of the free and the home of the brave!*

But was the fighting worth the horrible price? Before this question can be completely answered, I want to take you with me on a journey to the Philippines. As was mentioned earlier, I have been back more than forty times, and as is my custom each time, I visit the beautiful Manila American Cemetery and Memorial at Fort Bonifacio near Manila. It is a hallowed shrine standing as a grim reminder that the economic cost of the war is nothing compared to the cost in lives of those who gave their all.

You'll have to forgive my emotions. Just seeing this place and the American flag brings on tears, as the war comes back to me in vivid color. It's like turning a scar into an open wound!

The shrine is situated just outside of Manila. This is the largest in size of all the cemeteries that were built, and are maintained in both Europe and Asia by the United States Government. The grassy burial area is the final resting place for 17,206 soldiers, sailors, and marines, who gave their lives on the battlefields of the South Pacific and the Philippines. Each grave has a shining white marble cross or Star of David.

There are 152 acres of gently rising ground. At the highest point of the cemetery is the Memorial Chapel in the middle of two half-circles with marble columns, which stretch out for about one hundred meters in each direction. In these, the fifty U.S. states are identified, and on the columns are inscribed the names of those missing in action from each state. The total shocking number is 36,279!

Visiting this place is a once-in-a-lifetime experience for most people. For some, including myself, each visit is a ritual. An example of those who come often is a woman in our organization, who has spent twenty-eight years in the Philippines. Why did she come to this country? To be near her father. His name is one of those listed as missing in action! She comes to rest her hand on the column that bears his name, prays, and wonders where his final resting place might be. Throughout her life she has struggled with the very things with which I have struggled, especially the cost of the war.

This cemetery does not represent all those who gave their lives, including thousands of Filipinos. There were many replacement soldiers who joined our company, who died and/or were wounded, and we never even knew their names. When I returned to the Philippines in 1953 as a missionary, most of the thirty-two men from my company who made the initial landing and were killed in the battle for Luzon were buried here. However, relatives had the choice of leaving the body in the Manila cemetery or having it shipped home. My uncle was one of those who asked for the body of his son Lieut. Robert Holsinger to be sent home. My cousin was killed in Peleliu Island, which is one of the Palau Islands just east of Mindanao.

Within ten years from the end of the war, only two of the bodies of my comrades remain here—Claude Bunce and Lewie Hay (real names)—because they were orphans.

First Sergeant Claude Bunce was the first man from our company to die on Philippine soil. He lies at Plot A, Row B, Grave 85. Each time I come back I make it a point to visit his grave, place my hand on his marble cross, and make a recommitment of my life to God, my heavenly Father. Just give me a minute so I can kneel, and pray one more time…

The author visiting on October 28, 1998 the
Manila American Cemetery and Memorial at
the grave of First Sargeant Claude Bunce,
the first man from his company to die in the
Philippines.

I always leave his grave with mixed emotions. On the one hand my heart is heavy because of his rejection of God. (See chapter 5, "Lupao Town—First Battle".) At the same time I have hope. Perhaps in his dying moments on the rice field near Lupao, he cried out to the Lord for mercy and salvation.

The other orphaned comrade, Lewie Hay, rests on the far side, Plot H, Row 8, Grave 93. He was a big, simple man over six feet tall and quite heavy, who made a very large target for the enemy. Often he would joke, "Some day I'll have to get down real low, and I won't be able to do it." He was naive in many ways, which made the men of the company ridicule him, but to me he was a special friend. He often sought me out for talks. One of his frequent questions was: "I have no place to call home—what do I do after the war is over?" These conversations usually ended with tears streaming down his cheeks. The other men called him "Big Hay." But I gave him my own personal nickname of "Little Chum," which whenever he heard it always turned his morbid moments into laughter.

Lewie had all kinds of questions about the Bible and God. I encouraged him to accept God as his heavenly Father, and put his trust in Him. One of his favorite verses from the Bible that I had shared with him was Psalms 27:10, "Though my father and mother forsake me, the Lord will receive me." This gave him a glimmer of hope. A sniper's bullet sent him into eternity, as he sat alone on the edge of his foxhole. The little New Testament found in his pocket gave me hope that he is now with the Father in heaven.

So was the war worth it? With a resounding shout I say, "Yes," especially when I think of the choice our two countries faced—tyranny or freedom!

Not only was the war worth the sacrifice, but for me it made the whole experience worthwhile. I took home a treasure! As I struggled with the war, and the death and the maiming of comrades, something like a quiet whisper was spoken to my mind and heart. As I grappled with my hatred and anger of "the enemy," the words of Jesus and His life and death began to take hold of me. I knew He was one person who could enter into my feelings and pain. Eventually His crucifixion convinced me that there was no way that my pain could ever have equaled His. And yet His attitude toward His enemies was amazing.

As I moved along after the war, Jesus' words from the cross would come to me over and over again, "…Father, forgive them, for they do not know what they are doing" (Luke 23:34). Again I would hear his words in my heart: "And when you stand praying, if you hold anything against anyone, forgive him, so that your Father in heaven may forgive you your sins" (Mark 11:25).

But the one verse I could never escape from was: "But I tell you: Love your enemies and pray for those who persecute you, that you may be sons of your Father in heaven…" (Matthew 5:44). The thing that bothered me most was the way that Jesus personalized the enemy, using words like *your*, *mine*, and *my*.

God was constantly prompting me in my innermost being to do what Jesus did. But it would take a long time before I could forgive "my" enemy, the Japanese. I am grateful that God never gave up on me. The day came when I learned the secret of peace! It is forgiveness! This is my treasured gift from the war.

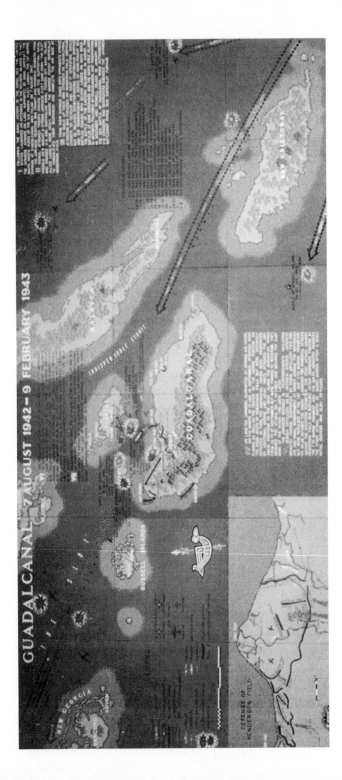

GUADALCANAL 7 AUGUST 1942 — 9 FEBRUARY 1943

1

EXCITEMENT ON BOARD— LAND IN SIGHT

After Guadalcanal and the Northern Solomon Islands[1] campaign, we were taken to New Zealand for rest and relaxation. In March 1944, we returned a second time to the island of New Caledonia[2] to get ready for our next campaign. In November 1944 we were on board ship again with no idea where we were going. Early in December we heard news that was received with mixed emotions—we would be landing in the Philippines![3]

The replacement soldiers joining us in New Caledonia, who had never been in combat before, were excited. Now each day meant that they were getting closer to being in the thick of battle. They itched for action, not realizing the terror of war. The old-timers—the veterans from Guadalcanal and the Northern Solomons—were silent and moody about the future. We figured that we had been "lucky" up until now, but the prospects of surviving another campaign seemed a bit remote.

Daily we heard reports about the progress of the war in both Europe and the Pacific. Now the hot news was the return of Gen. Douglas MacArthur, the joining of Filipino scouts and guerrillas with the American forces, the fight for the island of Leyte, and the destruction of the Japanese navy and air force.

As we came closer to the Philippines, there were more and more reports about the heroics of Filipino scouts and guerrillas. The former were Filipino members of the U.S. Army in the Philippines during peacetime. The latter were civilians who refused to submit to Japanese rule. (There were Filipino soldiers—about sixty thousand—who had been with the Americans in Bataan when the Philippines fell to the Japanese forces on April 9,1942. Many were able to escape into the jungles, and continued to fight against the Japanese until Gen. MacArthur's return in October 1944.)

Both groups were praised for their undercover activities and gathering of detailed information. It was amazing how much they knew about the Japanese—number of troops, ammunition and food supplies, where they stored equipment, number of tanks, and artillery pieces. Although this was great to hear, and eventually would prove invaluable in helping our forces save many lives, we were getting more and more irritable, wanting to get off this ship!

Early in January I woke up, and sensed that the ship was not moving. I went topside, and looked out. On one side was an armada of ships—as far as the eye could see—and on the other side, I saw land! We were told that we were looking at the area around Legaspi City in southern Luzon.

That evening there was excitement! Under cover of twilight Filipino scouts came on board to brief our commanders. We learned that they had been fighting the Japanese ever since the invasion of their homeland in early 1942. We looked in awe at these brave men, who had literally battled the Japanese with their bare hands. Just having the presence of a couple of these men on board stirred the emotions in us all. We were eager to join in the fight!

The scouts had maps for our officers, targeting Japanese bases, vital enemy supply routes, and concentration of forces.

On the 11th of January, 1945, we headed for shore...

...and landed at Lingayen Beach on the island of Luzon.

This information eventually was shared over the ship's intercom with us soldiers, after the scouts had left.

Later in the afternoon of the next day, as dusk began to settle in, the scouts were let down over the side of the ship into small rubber boats. We pressed toward the railing just to get a glimpse of them, as they slipped away into the darkness.

The critical information from the various scouts, who had joined ours and other ships, was shared with the high command, and this in turn enabled Gen. MacArthur to come up with a strategy. The plan was to trick the enemy into thinking that we would be landing a massive force in the south near the vicinity of Legaspi City. Gen. MacArthur hoped this would draw part of the Japanese army away from Manila and the foothills just beyond San Jose del Monte, and lure them into Central Luzon plain.[4]

We would wait until Filipino scouts, who were tracking the enemy's movements, reported that the Japanese had taken the "bait" about a Legaspi landing. With this information the ships would move out under cover of darkness, go around the mouth of Manila Bay, and head north to Lingayen Gulf. The troops would storm ashore, establish a perimeter, and then move quickly to encounter the enemy in the Central Luzon plain.

The strategy worked. It was January 10 when an armada of ships—literally hundreds of them—carrying units of the Sixth Army arrived in the gulf. Those of us in the Twenty-fifth Division spent the day on deck, watching the bombardment by our battleships and cruisers of the shore and hills. Especially exciting was to watch two *kamikaze*—suicide planes—trying to hit one of our battleships. The planes went down into the water trailing ribbons of smoke.

That evening it was announced that we would go ashore the next day! The days of boredom and monotony were over, but the work was just beginning.

Along with trying to get used to walking on land again, we worked night and day unloading critical supplies of equipment, ammunition, and food. While some worked at unloading ships, others were furiously digging foxholes, and preparing fortifications for safety. Not only were we shelled by enemy artillery from the hills, but there was also the constant threat of air raids. After two weeks of diving for cover at the sound of air raid sirens, we swept the last Japanese planes from the skies. We would not see another enemy plane for the duration of the war.

LIBERATION OF THE PHILIPPINES
20 OCTOBER 1944–15 AUGUST 1945

2

LIBERATION— BITTER AND SWEET

When we stormed ashore on the morning of January 11, 1945, there was no resistance. In a matter of hours Filipinos with tattered clothes, half-starved bodies, haggard and drawn faces began to emerge from hiding. The joy of liberation had begun.

The only thing that interrupted the celebration was the intermittent artillery shelling coming from Japanese big guns dug in on the hillsides. The roar of the huge shells sounded like freight trains passing overhead, and sent soldiers and Filipinos diving for cover. Some shells hit critical targets of fuel and ammunition, sending pillars of smoke into the sky. But casualties were light, and losses in goods were minimal.

It wasn't long before our navy had knocked out the guns on the hills, and brought peace to the beach. After a few days of quietness the war seemed a million miles away, and we enjoyed the beauty of the beach, and interacted with the people.

The natives, as the Filipinos were initially called, and the American soldiers, who were called "Joe," had quite a time getting acquainted. We stared at each other, laughed at each other, had fun together trying to communicate. It was one big party.

At first the American soldiers had no money. However, their pockets were loaded with candy for distribution and/or trade. Food rations and extra uniforms were great barter items also. Filipinos brought out coconuts, bananas, papayas, and Japanese money (occupation scrip) called "funny money." This proved to be in great demand as a souvenir for the GIs (another name for the American soldiers.) In just a few days the local people were trading souvenirs the likes of bolo knives and seashell necklaces. In the game of bartering, there were little circles of GIs and Filipinos trying to communicate with each other to make deals. There were hundreds of these "classes in English" going on everyday.

Division Headquarters were set up in the schoolhouse in San Jacinto. Carabao (water buffalo) carts began appearing, and hundreds of Filipinos came out of the hills for safety behind the American lines.

Accounts of mistreatment, torture, and depravities began to pour in. The occupation by the Japanese army was ugly and devilish. Soldiers from the U.S. Army staff were assigned to gather eyewitness accounts with one purpose in mind. The enemy army and the soldiers would be prosecuted to the full extent of the law. Even in a lifetime one doesn't forget such horrible and atrocious acts handed out by the enemy.

It was a special event for every "GI Joe," as we were affectionately called, to give assistance. It always brought a smile to the face of us soldiers, who had the privilege of rescuing these dear people. There was the young lady who emerged from the wooded area, who looked about sixteen years of age. She would be one of the many who would give a similar testimony. She was attractive but her hair was matted and she was covered with grime. She wanted to be clean, and she was hungry. There was a special office and area where people like this could bathe, be fed and clothed.

She began to pour out her heart. As she talked there were both tears of anger and tears of joy. Her hatred for the Japanese

Division Headquarters set up at San Jacinto Schoolhouse...

...and Division Artillery set up across the road

was understandable. Her joy of being liberated was beyond expression. All she could do was weep, as she realized she was set free. She had been raped repeatedly. The occupation officers turned their heads and ignored her cries for help, as the enemy foot soldiers had their fun with her body.

A mother with anguish and rage told of her baby being bayoneted. Her testimony was typical. The soldiers would enter a village, and at random would pull babies from their mother's arms, and destroy the child before the horrified eyes of the mother and other villagers.

The Japanese warning was always the same: "We'll be back, and if we find anyone cooperating with the guerrillas and/or Americans, the punishment will be twice as severe next time!"

The people would try to hide food and possessions but the Japanese searches were relentless. Oftentimes the cry of a baby would reveal a hiding place. The price would be beyond belief— whole families would be killed, and all they owned confiscated.

The enemy kept coming back and the same treatment was carried out. There was little questioning, and no chance to answer trumped-up charges. Every visit meant anguish and often death. The ultimate Japanese goal was to crush the spirit of the Filipinos, and bring them under complete subservience.

It was hard to believe that an enemy soldier would have the crudeness, lack of compassion, and no shame to cut off the breast of a nursing mother! Witnesses said that her screams would live with them forever.

Another woman came forward to testify that her pregnant sister had been stripped. She stood naked and quivering before her tormentors. Then a soldier with his bayonet ripped open her stomach. The final terror was that in her dying moments no one was allowed to go near her to give her comfort. She died alone as the enemy looked on with satisfaction.

A little boy told of hiding under a thatched hut when Japanese soldiers entered his village. He watched as the soldiers talked in hushed tones with his father. Then without warning a soldier slipped in behind the father, and with a swish of his meter-long samurai sword almost cut his father in two. The enemy left with the man dying in a pool of blood.

The enemy had stripped both men and women of their clothing, and in exchange had given them pieces of burlap (a fabric made of hemp or jute called *sako*) for covering. The irony of this "clothing exchange" was that the Japanese made every-one buy the burlap with Japanese scrip—the worthless money which had been paid to the Filipinos previously for their rice. This rough clothing caused itching and welts all over the body. It was almost too painful to wear, but they had nothing else to cover their nakedness.

In contrast to the enemy there was the American army dis-cipline that would protect women! (Yes, even Japanese women were protected after we invaded their homeland.) We all knew that this was the "unwritten" law—treat women with respect and dignity.

A good example of this was when a GI tried to get fresh with a Filipina, the first week we were on the beach. He had grabbed her, and pulled her into a clump of bushes. As he tore off her clothes, she screamed for help. In a matter of minutes other soldiers came to her rescue and set her free.

The soldier was court-martialled for conduct unbecoming of a soldier, and the army made an example out of him. He was stripped of his sergeant's rank, put in a stockade for the dura-tion of the war, and eventually given a dishonorable discharge. It was a solemn warning to all of us to keep our morals high, and our emotions under control.

But there were fun things happening, too. The GIs needed laundry service and baths. The older Filipina women had the answer. They would take the men's uniforms, wash them, and return them wet! This had to be the procedure because the men never knew when they would be moving on. It would be a tragedy for a man to have to march without his pants on! So soldiers were happy to wait around in the nude, until the laundry was ready.

Another good sideline for the older women was the bathing solution. Men would take off all their clothes, and stand between two ration boxes. Then the women would mount the boxes with buckets of water, and dump it over their heads and on their bodies. This event was a profit maker—rations, chocolate bars, cigarettes—for the women, since there would be no American money available for some time. This was a great entertainment and sport for the local people, who turned out daily to watch the event!

Soon Filipino men were walking the dusty roads and encouraging soldiers to witness cockfights, a favorite pastime of the men, and join in the fun. It was a mystery where the cocks had been hidden during the Japanese occupation!

Christians in the U.S. forces, who would not be moving on into combat, began sharing the Gospel with the Filipinos. One high ranking officer gave permission to a group of enlisted men to use a "six-by-six" (a truck with three axles and ten wheels) as a broadcasting unit, and drive up and down the roads, inviting Filipinos and GIs to come to Gospel rallies. The music (some soldiers had brought along guitars and harmonicas) and the ministry was a morale-builder for everyone.

One officer believed that these get-togethers between soldiers and Filipinos was a goodwill venture that could create camaraderie between the soldiers and the local people. He was right. When the top officers saw the response of the people to this kind of an event, it encouraged commanders to let the GIs expand their efforts.

When I returned to the Philippines in later years, I met men—some pastors and Bible teachers—who had come to know the Lord because of those meetings on the beach of Lingayen Gulf. A close Filipino colleague from my own mission organization, who is also a recognized world leader in missions, is affectionately known as "Dr. Met" (Castillo).[1] He told me that his father had first heard about the Lord as a result of these meetings.

God was already making use of the war to bring about salvation and comfort to the Filipino nation. He was also giving many GIs a vision, which would eventually lead them to return as missionaries. The blessing side of the war was becoming a reality. I thought of Psalm 76:10: "Surely the wrath of men shall praise thee…" (KJV).

3

HARSH REALITY—
WE'RE AT WAR

With all the excitement and euphoria of being part of the liberation forces, it was hard to believe that there was a war going on. The sense of safety within the perimeter, which stretched for miles, gave us all a good feeling. Everything that moved outside of our perimeter area was the enemy, unless otherwise identified. This was both a fact and a reality.

It was not long after our landing that word came down from headquarters for patrols to be sent out daily. Each company commander would patrol a given area to make sure that there was no sign of the enemy coming within striking distance of our supply base. A patrol would consist of one or two squads (10-20 men).

The patrols went out faithfully each day. For the first ten days, there was sporadic contact with Filipinos, but no contact with the enemy. This kind of a daily experience was a dangerous one in that it caused the troops to relax.

And then it happened. It was another company's turn to patrol. A squad consisting of twelve men were to move forward for about two kilometers (one and one-quarter miles), search two villages, and return. By midafternoon concern began to mount because the squad had not reported in. There was an uneasy feeling that something had gone wrong. The company commander ordered a large group of men to go on a searching party.

As the contingent moved down the road and into a curve, they saw the carnage. Nobody will ever know what happened, except that all the men were killed. Not only that, their bodies had been stripped and searched, and their weapons and ammunition were confiscated. This meant that sometime in the future our own weapons and ammunition would be used against us. The worst thing of all happened to them, the soldier's dread—to be hit by the enemy so fast, and so suddenly that there was no chance to fire back. This news shook us all. It was a sobering reminder that the enemy was real.

Since the destroyed squad was from a company that was a part of another battalion, it meant that four or more companies from the regiment would have representative participation as an honor guard for our fallen comrades.

I was walking through our company area and minding my own business when there was a call from our First Sergeant: "Hey, Holsinger, I need a man to be a part of an honor guard. You got five minutes to catch the truck."

I grabbed my helmet and rifle and joined about fifteen other men on the back of a big truck. We rambled for a short distance and picked up a lieutenant, a chaplain, and a bugler.

We headed toward the town of Pozorrubio. Our destination was a junction of three roads that formed a triangle. One road went north to Bontoc, another went south toward Manila, and a third one turned off toward San Fernando (La Union). At the center of this was the temporary burial place. (Later, the bodies would be exhumed, and moved to a permanent cemetery.)

In the middle of the triangle, faithful Filipino partners had dug twelve graves. The tagged body bags were lined up neatly, awaiting the ceremony.

It was a very somber time. No one talked. We quietly received instructions from the lieutenant, who lined us alongside the graves and the bodies. The chaplain said a few words, which I didn't hear. I was too focused on the rubber body bags. The chaplain read Psalm 23 and that I heard, which gave me some comfort. It was then time for the salute.

The lieutenant called us to attention. Then came the commands: "Port arms. Shoulder arms. Ready, aim fire!" Our guns barked in unison. Then he called us to attention one more time. The bugler blew taps, and the ceremony was over.

We climbed onto the truck, and were on our way back to our companies. No one talked, but one could tell that there was lots of thinking going on. One thought was on every man's mind: "What, and who will be next?"

As we rode along, I saw the burial site fade in the distance. I thought of the uncertainty of tomorrow. I realized that trying to live a day at a time was too long a time frame. My only option was a step at a time. A Bible verse came to my mind, Psalm 37:23: "The steps of a good man are ordered by the Lord: and he delighteth in his way." (KJV). I told the Lord I wanted to be that kind of man.

I suddenly became homesick. My thoughts drifted back to home—the first time I saw my father cry as he heard the news about the attack on Pearl Harbor on December 7, 1941; he said, "Charley, this means you will have to go to war"; my mother's tears as we hugged, kissed, and said goodbye to each other, and I boarded a train for army active duty on January 1, 1943. Next I remembered our church—I could see myself sitting with my family. Tears welled into my eyes, and I wondered if I would ever see home again. At that moment a song came to my mind, which I had learned in church, and I began to sing it to myself:

> *Turn your eyes upon Jesus,*
> *Look full in His wonderful face,*
> *And the things of earth will grow strangely dim,*
> *In the light of His glory and grace.*[1]

With this song in my heart I felt better.

Individuals and groups of Filipinos came everyday to be interrogated, examined medically, and given food. The Japanese were quick to take advantage of this situation, and we soon learned another costly lesson.

A Japanese soldier gathered a number of Filipinos together and asked them to escort him to the American lines so he could surrender. This was great news for the Filipinos, and they were more than glad to participate.

But there was a sinister reason for this, which the Filipinos were not aware of. The enemy soldier was a *kamikaze*—a man on a suicide mission. The little band of men approached the perimeter and asked to be allowed to enter. It was very easy for a Japanese to disguise himself by wearing tattered clothing, and slip through the inspection. Also his skin color and facial features were somewhat similar to the Filipinos', which made it difficult for the GIs to identify him. Everyone was given a mere fleeting glance, and then waved into the perimeter.

They crossed the perimeter line and proceeded to the interrogation center. It was then the Japanese guy made his bold move. He was laced with dynamite, and he pulled the detonator cord. In an instant he blew himself and many others into eternity, and left many wounded and maimed.

It was a bitter lesson, which made us all itch to get the enemy in the sights of our rifles. My hatred and dislike for the enemy reached a new high. I burned with anger over the senseless loss of my fellow soldiers and our Filipino comrades.

For the first time I really had to grapple with the whole problem of war and killing. Earlier as a Christian, I had faced this experience as a "holy war." The Japanese were Shinto worshipers, and most of the Americans had some kind of a Christian leaning. In the Old Testament I understood clearly that God had allowed wars, especially just ones. And I felt that this war was justified. The Japanese were the aggressors, and punishment needed to be dished out. Furthermore, to the combat soldiers these were not people. They were more like rodents that needed to be destroyed.

At the same time I felt that the Filipinos suffered the same consequences as the Americans. We were in this together, to avenge ourselves, and finally to defeat an aggressor and a wicked enemy.

There was no question about it. I was one soldier ready to fight! It would not be long before the whole reality of war would engulf me, and I would know what it meant to be "face to face" with the enemy.

4

"DALTON'S ARMY"

The beachhead was secure. Now it was time for the infantry regiments—the 27th, 35th, and the 161st—in our division to seek and destroy the enemy. The 27th Infantry took the lead, going east through the towns of San Manuel and San Quentin. The 35th would go through Rosario[1], and the 161st would be in reserve.

The 27th next advanced into Imugan. Three days later excited talk swirled through the ranks and stirred our blood for battle. The word getting around was about the teamwork and the heroics of the "Wolf Hounds" (the nickname for the 27th Infantry) and the Filipino farmers. Later this combined group would affectionately be called "Dalton's Army," as a result of a battle at the little village of Pemienta, several kilometers away from Umingan.

Filipino intelligence reported that some enemy units would be abandoning Manila to move north to join Gen. Yamashita's forces in the mountains. At the same time guerrillas brought word that this was such a huge convoy, carrying both supplies and soldiers, that the Japanese were taking every precaution to make sure that nothing would hinder the success of the journey.

When Col. Dalton, commanding officer of the 27th, heard this news, he made a decision to act! He immediately ordered the artillery to zero in on a road junction about twenty kilometers away, through which the convoy must pass. But as he thought on the situation, he realized that if he were to be successful, soldiers needed to be there to assure complete victory.

The colonel came up with an ingenious plan to intercept the convoy at the road junction. But he had a problem. If he used trucks for transportation, the noise would alert any Japanese scouts. In the light of this he would enlist the services of the local Filipino farmers in the area together with their pack animals—horses and carabaos—to bring his men there.

The word spread quickly, and by noon of the next day there was a large assortment of farmers, carts (wagons), horses and carabaos eager and ready to carry about two hundred men and equipment to the area of the junction.

The time factor was now critical. A new report came in— they reckoned that the enemy convoy would reach the junction that very night! By early afternoon the animals and carts were packed and ready, and this strange adventure was underway.

Traveling via back roads and trails that only the farmers knew, "Dalton's Army" reached the drop-off area.

Equipment and men were quickly dispersed to nearby shaded areas to wait until the sun was about to set. The farmers were dismissed, and they retreated to high ground to watch and wait for what would happen in the darkness.

With evening coming on, the colonel had about three hours to get his men into position, and to set up his defenses. Foxholes were dug with dirt flying in all directions, as the perimeter was established with the road junction in the middle.

At about 10:00 P.M. a Filipino scout reported the convoy had so many soldiers that they would outnumber the colonel's forces. Now the concern was whether the Japanese had seen the activities of the afternoon. If our movement had been spotted, then the commander of the convoy could plan a surprise counterattack.

The colonel weighed his options. If there was an enemy counterattack, the main road would probably be abandoned, which in turn would mean the artillery and mortars would be useless. He and all of his men could be in jeopardy. In spite of the risk the colonel decided to stay with his original plan.

It was getting along toward midnight when the soldiers began to hear the rumbling of trucks. The showdown was approaching. Every man was alert. Tension mounted as the trucks moved slowly toward their rendezvous with death. As the sound of the trucks grew louder, Col. Dalton sent word along the line, telling the men to be patient. They were to hold their fire, until he gave a shout!

The trucks moved slowly to within one hundred meters, then seventy-five meters, then fifty meters—not a headlight was burning—the engines were now a roar. Twenty-five meters, and then the colonel gave a shout!

The first truck kept moving, and reached the edge of a foxhole before it was stopped. The roar of artillery, mortar shells, rifle and machine-gun fire was unbelievable. The enemy tumbled out from the back of trucks dazed, bewildered, and confused. Screaming filled the air, as some of the enemy charged our men, who cut them down with rifle fire. Firing was at point-blank range—it was almost impossible to miss. The bombardment was deafening, as artillery shells exploded and shook the earth. The sky was alive with fireworks and burning flares to expose the enemy.

And then in a matter of minutes there was unbelievable stillness that was punctuated every now and then by groans from the dying. For the rest of the night, the soldiers on the perimeter waited for the rays of the morning sun. When morning came, the soldiers assessed the damage and viewed the carnage. The enemy had been destroyed, and fifty or sixty trucks lay in ruin. Bits and pieces of men were mingled with twisted

One night a huge Jap convoy of tanks, infantry, and artillery on its way to Umingan roared into a barrio called Pemienta...

...so the 27th's roadblock, and bazooka men who were in the fields all along the highway, opened fire.

steel. Bodies were everywhere—some were whole, but others had legs and arms missing. The body count exceeded two hundred. In contrast, we had only a few minor injuries, and not one American lost his life.

So many Japanese died that bulldozer tractors had to be brought in to dig trenches to bury them. As the tractors prepared the makeshift graves, the farmers returned to help in the disposal of bodies, and to share in the spoils of war. Clothing and food supplies, along with anything else they could find, were their reward.

The victory was a great morale-builder for both the American soldiers and the Filipinos. The GIs and the Filipino team gained great status, as the word spread across the countryside.

Even though my outfit was not a part of this action, the news inspired and fired us up to get into the battle, and get the war over with.

As I write this book there are men and women, who live in the general vicinity of where this event took place, who tell this story with great embellishment and pride. Over the years, when I returned to the Philippines, I personally met Filipinos who were part of "Dalton's Army."

5

LUPAO TOWN— FIRST BATTLE

FIRST DAY

When this four-day battle would be over, the total experience for me would be like a North Star for the rest of my life—there would be no question about the reality of God and/or His protection and care.

Our battalion (about one thousand men) was strung out for miles, and was quietly moving along with about five meters between each soldier. This was the normal procedure for advancing across open territory. As we trudged along the dusty road under the brilliant sun, little did we know that our first battle was only hours away.

The road was nothing more than a ox-cart trail with deep ruts. With full packs on our backs, walking on uneven ground was awkward and difficult.

By noon it was blistering hot, and there was no shade. The heavy sweating made uniforms stick to our bodies, which added to the discomfort. Because of reports that the road might be

The 35th's march to Lupao was a long, hot one, and the road was mined as it approached the barrio.

mined, we stopped often. The anticipation of stepping on one of these land mines increased our tension and apprehension. Besides this, there was uncanny silence—no sound of any shooting—not even any distant explosions.

It was late in January when our Thirty-fifth Infantry Regiment (about three thousand men, see glossary), which was composed of three battalions, was poised for the assault on the town of Lupao. The reconnaissance report stated there were only a few Japanese stragglers, and that at the most we would encounter only small arms fire.

But there was a surprise. The First Battalion had been stymied from making a successful frontal assault. The new plan was for our battalion, the Third, to circle around the town, and come in from the opposite side. Company "K," of which I was a part, would lead the attack.

Everyone was awake by 4:00 A.M. By 6:30 A.M. the heat of the morning sun helped to intensify the emotional pressure. My stomach was as tight as a fighter's clenched fist—so tight I couldn't swallow food or water. (The best way to understand the tension is to squeeze your fist as tight as you can for fifteen minutes—that was my stomach.) My tongue was already parched by the strain. I took a sip from my canteen, but there was no relief.

As the scout or point man, I would be the first man out. My friend and buddy, Lou, would be right behind me. Glancing at him, I could see he was struggling, too. In silence we crouched by the roadside waiting for final instructions from our company commander.

In a moment like this, a soldier lives alone with his own thoughts and has lots of questions: *Is this my last day on earth? Will I live or die courageously? Will I make the right decisions?*

Along with the normal mental and emotional struggles, I had an overriding thought. This was an unusual situation, which added to my agony. Here we were: two close friends who would be facing uncertainty together. At the same time, ringing in my ears was the repeated reminder by our first sergeant: "You guys must go out, but you don't have to come back."

Lou and I had been thrown together in "K" Company, 35th Infantry Regiment back in New Zealand. Over the past year we had bonded; we appreciated each other. In every sense we were like brothers. We shared the beauty of many sunsets and always tried to focus on the positive side of life. He was Catholic and I was Protestant, but we shared a common faith in the reality of God and His Son, Jesus Christ.

We had long talks about God, life and death, families, and home. Many times our homesickness was so strong that tears choked out our words. Words were useless at times like that. We would sit in silence for long periods until we got control of our emotions. And we had talked about a situation like what we faced today, but we never thought it would ever happen.

The captain joined us for instructions, and jolted us back to reality. We were to move across the rice field. About two hundred meters away we could see a stream configuration that looked like a horseshoe. To the south end of the horseshoe opening was a bamboo thicket, and to the north—about one hundred meters—was a large clump of bushes. Our first objective would be the bamboo thicket. The artillery would lift at 7:05 A.M. Immediately we were to enter the bamboo. Simultaneously we would give a hand signal for the main body of soldiers to advance.

Pointing to the map, the captain gave one final instruction: "Stay clear of the left side of the stream. We will be dropping in mortar fire, and we don't want to hit you."

At about 6:45 A.M. came the command from First Sergeant Bunce, "Jump off!" These would be the last words that he would speak to us in this life.

Lou and I scrambled over the embankment and across the rice field. As we reached the vicinity of the bamboo, the artillery stopped. I gave a hand signal and looked back. The main body of troops were swarming out from their protected area. There was unusual quietness! The only thing I could hear and feel was my heart pounding in my throat.

Rather than making a frontal approach to the bamboo, I made the decision to go beyond it, and come in from the rear.

There was a slow-moving stream, and I followed it back to the bamboo.

About thirty meters from our objective, there was an ear-shattering explosion. Then another, which blew off my helmet, and left me stunned, and on my hands and knees in the stream. In an instant I thought, *Our mortars!* I staggered to my feet, and shouted to Lou, "Let's get out of here!"

We quickly ran north from the bamboo, across the open area toward our second objective, which was a clump of bushes about one hundred meters away, on the edge of the same stream. As we ran we heard explosions behind us.

We were steps away from protection when I dove for cover Then I heard a cry from Lou, who was about ten meters behind me, "I'm hit!"

I looked back. He was on the ground, writhing in agony.

Suddenly it was as though the whole earth came to life! The chatter of machine guns, tank cannons, and rifle fire filled the air. The battle was on!

I cried out, "Oh God, help!" I crawled out on my stomach, grabbed Lou, and with superhuman strength, wiggling and tugging at his uniform, I was able to drag him to the safety of the streambed.

I tried to shout above the noise of the gunfire to our troops, "Send a medic, quick!" It was no use. The main body was now pinned down by crossfire from two machine-gun nests, and a fusillade from enemy tank guns.

Looking back toward the bamboo thicket, I could see the turret of an enemy tank. Just moments before, Lou and I were moving toward the mouth of the tank's cannon! The amazing thing is that both shots fired at us missed!

But that didn't help our present situation. Lou had sustained a two-inch-wide gash from a fragment of an exploding shell on his back near the heart, and was bleeding profusely. The back of his uniform was oozing blood. I tore off his shirt. My hands were drenched in blood, as I tried to find the wound. I knew that it would be just a matter of time before he bled to death. I found the hole!

With the battalions squeezing in from both sides of town, it was necessary for the artillery to fire dangerously close to our own men.

I took out my first-aid packet, which every soldier carried. As I applied pressure, I cried out to the Lord to help me stop the bleeding. He answered!

Lou was in deep shock, and lapsed in and out of consciousness. I thought he was dying. All I could do was leave him in the Lord's hand. In the meantime my growing concern was a chattering Jap machine gun that was just a few yards away, and firing at our troops. About two hours later we were able to knock it out with grenades and rifle fire, and the medics were able to rescue Lou.

A sergeant shouted to me to join the rest of the company on the attack. As I moved across the original open area and went back toward the bamboo, a machine gun opened fire, and I hit the ground. Every time I moved there was a burst of fire, but I was just low enough so the bullets cleared my body. It's a strange feeling to suddenly realize you are in the enemy sights, and the only target. My first thought was to run. Fear screamed at me: *Get out of here!* I grabbed the earth with both of my hands to keep from getting up, as I fought the urge to run.

I was on my back looking up into the blazing tropical sun and wishing for death. The heat was almost unbearable, and I longed to get at my canteen at the backside of my belt, but I couldn't roll over.

By midmorning our men knocked out the machine-gun nest, and I was able to join the main body of troops, who were now engaged in a battle with three tanks that were dug in just to the south of the bamboo.

Molotov cocktails—bottles with highly explosive liquid that smashed against a tank, sticking to the metal, and then burning intensely—and bazookas joined in the action. From my vantage point all I could do was lie on my stomach and watch the battle. If I used my rifle, I would be firing over the heads of my own troops. Besides that, rifles were useless against tanks.

I spotted our lieutenant shouting for bazooka fire, as he moved on his stomach to within about three meters of the first tank, and smashed it with a cocktail.

When the enemy heard the word *bazooka*, they began abandoning their tank shouting, "Bazooka, bazooka!" (Evidently they already had learned the destructive power of this weapon.) As they climbed from the tank turrets, they were picked off by our rifle and machine-gun fire.

The three tanks were destroyed, and the fire from the Molotov cocktails left them slowly smoldering in the late afternoon. Their crew were dead.

It would soon be twilight, and we regrouped to dig in for the night. We had taken the open field, and my foxhole would be alongside the bamboo thicket, not far from one of the smoldering tanks.

One of the dead enemy was hanging half out of his tank turret, and was slowly cooking. The odor of burning flesh wafted through the still evening air. The smell was sickening, but it was a good feeling to see the enemy in such a condition.

It had been a bloody day. Casualties in our company (of about two hundred men) were six dead, and seventeen wounded. The casualty count from other companies was uncertain. I received a note two days later from my friend Dick Lawrence, company clerk of "B" Company, that our friend Frank from Headquarters Company, who had conducted Bible studies with the chaplain, had been killed this same day.

I was still alive. But I was disappointed. I hadn't fired a shot! The captain came by and commended me for a job well done. He said, "You did the right thing. You discovered the enemy!"

I didn't know whether Lou lived or died, and wouldn't know until four months later!

That night the word was passed down the line about our company's dead and wounded. When I heard the names of the ones who died, I was overcome with sadness.

My mind took me back to July 29, 1944 on the island of New Caledonia. Colonel Larson, the commanding officer of our regiment, called together two companies at a time. He gave information that in a short while we would all be going into combat again. Then he said, "We will have heavy fighting. We will all go, but many of us will not come back. I want you men to make sure that you are right with God. I have given the chaplains instruction to be available for counseling." We were dismissed, and there was a lot of heavy thinking going on.

The chapel was a tent in the middle of the regimental area, where I often went just to be quiet and alone. On this night, after the colonel's talk, I went there with heaviness of heart, and with a great inward struggle. I knew that God was trying to get through to me.

The issue was my future and my inward peace. I told the Lord that I would go any place, and do anything He wanted me to do except preach and/or go to a cold country like Alaska. But my restrictions on God left me with no peace.

Finally, after a long time of struggling, I gave in. I prayed, "Lord, here is my life. I'll be and do whatever You want of me." Suddenly I sensed the presence of God, and it scared me! I was frantic. I knew that I had made the right choice because of the peace in my heart, but I didn't know what to do! So I ran out of the chapel and headed back to my company and my tent, which I called home.

There were six guys talking about the usual—girls, gambling, and what they would do when they got home. We were friends, and knew each other well. We had been in foxholes together, and from time to time had shared our hopes and dreams with one another.

Now I interrupted them. "Men," I said, "tonight I made the decision of my life. I told God that I would do and be whatever He wanted of me—even be a preacher!"

There was silence as they stared at me. After what seemed like an eternity, one of the men responded, "If you were a preacher, what would you preach?"

This invitation gave me an opportunity to share what had happened to me that night. Along with this, I also gave them a brief definition of what it meant to be a Christian. Then I said, "What about you guys? What's your decision? You heard the colonel this afternoon!"

Again there was silence. Finally, First Sergeant Bunce, who knew exactly what I was talking about, since he was one of those who censored every letter I wrote home, got up and said, "That's stuff for kids." And he walked out. (He was a good leader, the highest-ranking non-commissioned officer in our company, and respected by us all. He was one of those orphans who wanted to improve his lot in life. So when he was fourteen years old, he lied about his age and joined the peacetime army. Now he was nineteen, just four months older than I.) Then one by one the others left, and I was all alone.

But in my heart there was tremendous joy. I knew that I had made the right decision, and I thanked the Lord for the peace. I took out my Bible, and on the blank empty page in the back wrote: "July 29, 1944. Through Jesus Christ I claim these now: 1) I will stay with the company, and go into combat as a scout. (A chaplain friend of mine had asked me to be his assistant, which would take me away from the company and any front-line fighting); 2) The Lord will help me do something in the next campaign that will be a testimony to the whole company; 3) Let me see my mother again. 'The battle is on, forward to the attack!'" But I knew that these kinds of requests would have to be miracles, as I faced the unknown future. Whether I lived or died in the next battlefield, wherever that would be, I had the assurance that the Lord was in charge of my life, and I had peace.

Now it was about eight months later in Luzon, and at the end of our first day in battle. I was shocked as I once again reviewed the names of those who were dead. The six men killed were the ones who had been in my tent on the night of July 29, 1944 on the island of New Caledonia, when I shared my exciting experience with God.

SECOND DAY

The day started out like the first one. Where we dug in represented the front line of battle. We would jump off from there to move into the village.

The sound of enemy tank engines retreating toward the center of town put us on early alert. It meant that sooner or later, we would face another heavy encounter. Rather than trying to bring our tanks into the battle—we had lost two the day before—the decision was made that the infantry would move forward until stopped by tank fire. Then we would use bazookas and Molotov cocktails.

Once again I would be the lead scout. Henry, a new partner, would replace Lou. The plan would be to leave our packs in the foxholes, and return to them in the evening. It was our hope that the enemy would be finished off before the day was over.

The captain called Henry and me over for a consultation. We joined him under a tree behind a crumbling cement wall. Immediately in front of us was a half-standing house. We could see a small yard through a large hole in the wall of the house. About twenty-five meters away at one extreme end of the yard was what looked like a clothesline pole.

The instructions from the captain were short but clear: "Holsinger, crawl over the rubble, and keep low. Enter through the hole, cross the yard, and stop at the pole. You can see bushes immediately beyond the pole. Be alert. Wait at the pole for further instructions. Henry, after you get through the hole, stop. You stay under the house, and give protection to Holsinger."

The captain looked at his watch, and said: "Jump-off time will be in about thirty minutes." That would be about 8:00 A.M.

Henry and I sat there, and talked briefly. Although the sound of enemy engines had ceased, the thought of tanks was uppermost in our minds. But right now our only focus was on the twenty-five meters that was immediately ahead.

The command came to move out. I cautiously went forward and made my way toward the pole, expecting enemy fire at every step. I knew the enemy was out there somewhere, and that they would be the first to fire. If there was a chance, I would fire back. But, being this close, it would mean that my chances of survival would be minimal. I knew that only a miracle would save me. I offered a silent prayer.

I reached the pole and quickly flattened out on my stomach—watching and listening. In front of me lay a path running from right to left, and beyond that about ten meters away was thick underbrush, which limited my forward view. I had a clear view of the path in both directions—from right to left—for about twenty-five meters, and then there were bushes.

After about an hour, I decided to sit up and lean against the pole. It sure felt good to change my position. I stretched my legs out and they touched the path. My rifle was across my lap. The silence was unusual.

After sitting for a couple more hours in the morning sun, I was beginning to feel drowsy and was fighting sleep. Suddenly movement to my right brought me to full alert. Out from the bushes stepped an unarmed Japanese soldier! We frightened each other—he jumped, and I froze with amazement! By the time I swung my rifle around to fire, he was gone as quickly as he appeared. But the fact that I had been spotted made me realize that I was now being watched. I was wide awake now, recognizing my danger!

While I was contemplating the situation and trying to still my rapidly beating heart, I heard a call. (This would be my salvation, but I wouldn't find out the full significance of it until the next day.) It was from Henry: "Hey, Chuck. The captain says retreat." With that good word, I wheeled around, and began crawling as fast as I could, expecting a shot at any moment. In a matter of seconds I was behind the wall, and in the presence of the captain. I gave him my report and rejoined my squad.

In the afternoon there was a change in plans. Another company moved into our foxholes, and we were assigned to a reserve position. Our company would guard the battalion aid station.

Faithful Filipinos, who were part of the aid station staff, joined us as stretcher-bearers. From other areas around the town, they brought in the wounded and the dying. Daily they risked their lives to rescue our fallen comrades. They did not carry weapons, but proudly wore the white armband with the red cross. By their quick and daring action on the field of battle, they got the wounded to medical assistance at a minimum amount of time. They saved many a GI from death.

The tragedy was that the Japanese targeted these heroes and tried to kill them. This they did in defiance of the Geneva War Convention Declaration, which protects first-aid men, and which the Japanese had signed. But the enemy tried as much to wipe out our Filipino comrades as they did the U.S. soldiers.

As I surveyed the scene, I noticed among the wounded a Filipino and an American soldier lying on stretchers next to each other, silently dying. The doctor had tagged them as "no hope for survival." The soldier was in battle fatigues, and the Filipino was in tattered clothing with a red cross armband. As to importance, both were significant, and both had equal rank. I watched their blood drip onto the soil, mix together, and then sink slowly into the ground. They had both given their all for freedom. At that moment and forever, I would see Filipinos and Americans as "blood brothers" in more ways than one.

Hanging around and watching the doctors trying to save the wounded and dying made me realize the price of war. The real cost is when one starts counting the bodies of fellow soldiers and Filipinos in the rubber body bags.

The day was almost over. Tonight we would occupy the holes around the aid station with two men to a hole. My partner would be a bazooka man. The sun was beginning to set when shouts came down the line from the men who were closest to the town: "Tanks coming!" Sure enough, down the road at full speed came a medium tank, its roar accompanied with guns blazing, which sent all of us scrambling to the shelter of our holes.

Jim, the bazooka man, had loaded his weapon earlier in the day just in case. He grabbed it, and I grabbed my rifle and started shooting. My bullets were just a joke, as they bounced off the tank as though nothing had happened. Jim was ready, took careful aim, and fired. There was a swishing sound, and I traced the bazooka rocket as it hit the tank tread. There was an immediate explosion. The tank started to spin in a circle and then rolled over on its side into a ditch. The turret flew open, and out came the occupants with pistols blazing. They were finished off quickly with our rifle fire. The body search of the men from the tank showed that they were ranking Japanese officers—one a colonel—who were trying to escape from the inevitable surrender of the town.

THIRD DAY

The men from the company who relieved us in the town were in for a horrible surprise. They spread out in a skirmish line (spread out in a long horizontal fashion) down the path—right along where I had been sitting by the post yesterday. The word was given to move out across the path. In seconds there was a tremendous burst from machine guns that caught our men in the crossfire. The company commander, along with a number of his men died instantly. The enemy was waiting for us to cross the path!

Later that day some of us were assigned to clean up the carnage. It would mean removing the "Nip" bodies, and destroying their machine guns and ammunition.

Upon examining the well-camouflaged gun emplacements and checking out the firing lanes, I discovered that yesterday I was in the corner of the sights all morning long! It was especially true when I sat up, leaned against the pole, and stretched out my legs onto the path. They were watching my every move. The bullets that cut the company to shreds could have ended my days on earth! But they never fired at me. They were waiting for a bigger target, and their patience was rewarded. But once again, God had spared my life!

In the afternoon, the troops pushed on into town. The cannon fire and bazookas thundered, as enemy tanks returned

The Medics set up aid stations as near the front as possible.

the fire. The enemy was pushed into a small pocket, and rather than risk any more men by another frontal assault, the commanding officer called for artillery fire to pulverize what was left of the resistance.

Our company moved around the town, and took up positions to secure the opposite side from which we had attacked. I was placed next to a large tree, which meant tough digging. Immediately next to me was a machine-gun crew—two men and their gun would occupy the same hole. For these two men, digging a hole for themselves and their weapon was no small project. However, today they were fortunate. Their location for digging was on the soft soil of a rice paddy, and they did a beautiful job!

My hole was a different story. The ground was hard, and the roots of the great tree were a constant obstacle. I struggled for a couple of hours, and then decided that I would dig no more. The hole was only about a foot deep, but I thought that that shallow protection would be adequate. Besides I was exhausted.

FOURTH DAY

Early the next day, our captain decided to move the machine gunners to a more strategic spot. It would mean that they would have to dig a new hole. Cursing, they packed up and moved on.

This was a perfect opportunity for me! I abandoned my small, shallow hole and moved into their vacant one, and prepared for a relaxing morning. I dug the hole a little deeper, made a mound of dirt for my pillow, and smoothed out a cardboard ration box for my bed pad.

About fifteen minutes later, I realized I had made a mistake. By digging deeper and because of the rice paddy I had hit water! This meant that I would have to move out. Disappointed I reluctantly packed up, and moved back to my original hole. I stretched out contemplating my misfortune.

Moving through sniper country is always a tedious job...

...and enemy fire makes you glad to embrace the hard bosom of "Mother Earth."

I was no sooner settled in than the artillery started to pound the town. The shells went winging over our heads, crashing into enemy positions. And there I was lying on my back, looking at the tree, being very disappointed that I was not in the bigger foxhole with more protection.

Suddenly there was a flash. I caught sight of something striking the tree above me to the right. This was accompanied by a whirling sound. A faulty artillery shell (called a short round) had hit the tree, bounced down on my right side—about two meters from my hole, flew up and over me, and landed upside down in the foxhole I had vacated, on the very spot where I had made my dirt pillow! All three non-direct hits—glancing off the tree, landing upside down next to my hole, and then coming to rest on its back end in the hole where my head had been—didn't detonate the shell!

An artillery officer had to retrieve the short round, dig a hole, and then detonate the shell! When he saw where I was in relation to the hits, he said: "Hey, soldier you are one lucky guy to be alive. I sure don't know why it didn't go off. If that shell had exploded in any one of those places, you would have been dead. It just didn't land right."

Then he said to me, "Are you married?"

I said, "No, why?"

He said with concern: "I'm married and have two kids at home, and I have to pick up that shell and carry it away. I just hope to God it doesn't go off when I pick it up!" His face was pale, as he tried to decide how to handle the problem.

With that information, I didn't stay to watch! I took off for cover behind a big tree, and waited on my stomach. Fortunately the officer was able to retrieve the shell and take care of it without incident.

By noon the battle of Lupao was over. We had knocked out twenty-six tanks, and only God knows how many of the Japanese soldiers were destroyed. Once again God in an amazing way had spared my life!

6

THE BIBLE IS FOR REAL

In the battlefields of Luzon were sown the seeds that eventually bore fruit in my life and ministry. These influenced my perspective forever. The bad side of the war was the emotional pressure, deplorable living conditions, homesickness, anguish by day, terror by night, and the uncertainty of life. Death stalked every step, every day, every hour, every second. On the good side were the lessons learned.

After the battle of Lupao we experienced small encounters. We moved quickly to Cabanatuan City, and turned north to San Jose. In both of these cities the Japanese had abandoned large amounts of goods. This was a good sign. The pressure of our advancing army robbed the enemy of precious supplies.

Capturing these two places enabled us to cut permanently the route of escape (Highway 5) to the mountains for the Japanese stragglers, who were coming from as far away as Manila. In these small groups there was not enough concentration of the enemy to launch major attacks on us. However they were persistent in slowing us down with harassing tactics, which cost us a number of lives.

As I looked at my circumstances, I had two options. I could curse, gripe, and complain—or bless, give thanks, and rejoice. For example, there were the sunsets. In the Philippines these are spectacular, especially looking at them from across open expanses of water. I have been told that the volcanic ash in the air makes the sky come alive with beauty. The colors change dramatically as the sun goes down. I tried to be grateful for this.

Early on during our time on the beach perimeter, it was a joy to watch the sun sink into the Lingayen Gulf, and beyond into the South China Sea. But once the sun was gone, darkness settled in quickly. Being near the equator means there is almost no twilight and no lingering shadows.

Moving away from the beach and into the battle area had changed my perspective. Instead of evening being a time of enjoyment, it became an ugly spectacle because it signaled the night!

There is no terror that can compare with a soldier's nights on the front line. Even though around a perimeter every third soldier is awake, it gives little comfort, little security, little reason to be thankful. There are just too many things that happen that put a man's nerves on edge, and rob him of any peace.

If nothing else there was the struggle to maintain one's sanity. The men on guard are your only hope. They spend their time staring into the darkness, trying to discern between normal and abnormal sounds, and wondering whether to shoot or not to shoot. If one shoots and there is no enemy, it still could mean jeopardy. The flash of a firing rifle could reveal one's position.

After being on guard and looking into the darkness for an hour or more, it seems that things are moving, even though they are not! Nerves become taut with anxiety, as one thinks about the responsibility that rests on his shoulders. He must stay awake. To doze off even for a few minutes could mean death or at best, a court martial. It is pure agony trying to stay awake after a day of fighting, or a long patrol.

Being under severe battle stress during the day often means that sleep is impossible. The body cries out for rest, but the nerves just don't respond. The soldier must take his turn to be awake—at least three hours every night.

Just thinking about duty at night is stress enough to drive men crazy. Some men crack up and have to be subdued, tied up, and gagged until morning. Some would never be normal again.

I got to the place where I could not rest, even though it was time to sleep. My tiredness made me stagger like a drunken man when I tried to walk. I thought I was going crazy. The top of my head felt like the lid on a boiling pot, ready to blow off. The pressure made my brain feel like it was going to explode. I desperately needed sleep.

I knew I had to do something. I cried out to the Lord for help, but heaven seemed to be closed. I kept asking myself questions that I couldn't answer: *If there is an attack will the men on guard respond quickly enough? Will I have a chance to fight back? Will I freeze in the midst of flying bullets? If I die, Lord, will You let me do so firing with my rifle?*

In my agony, suddenly from the "curse of darkness" came a new reality of light! One afternoon, as we were taking a ten-minute break sitting along a dusty road, I pulled my little New Testament out of my pocket, and decided that I would read through the Psalms during the next couple of days. At first I was just seeing words with no meaning. As I read I was unaware and oblivious that God was trying to get through to me.

During that short break, the Lord began to answer my prayer. I got as far as Psalm 4:8 when the Lord turned on the light! "I will both lay me down in peace, and sleep; for thou, Lord, only makest me dwell in safety" (KJV). That became one of my foxhole verses, and my salvation.

I said: "OK, Lord, it is Your responsibility to take care of me. Whether I live or die, I'm going to sleep. I'll either see You in the morning, or I'll see You later in heaven. Good night." I never lost sleep again!

In the next few days, all of us would be tested almost beyond endurance, and I needed some further assurance. We had been losing men at a frightening rate, and our supply line had been cut off by the enemy, which meant that we would have to be supplied by airdrop. Our survival would depend on no low hanging clouds. On top of this there was bad news. A typhoon (tropical storm) was moving in on us. Up to this time *typhoon* was simply a word that had very little meaning for any of us. However, this storm would change our perspective. It would practically render us helpless before the enemy.

We reached a knoll with no trees. Earlier in the day what little grass was there was burned off by us earlier to expose the enemy. Before any advance could be made our supply line had been cut off by them. Our only choice—stay on the hill. The order came down the line to dig in, and dig deep for our own safety. In other words, it looked like our situation was a precarious one, and we would be there for an extended period of time.

Word passed around the perimeter that we needed to take extra precautions because of the expected winds and rain. As usual we dug our foxholes and put up our ponchos (a rain coat that looked like a cape, which could serve as a tent covering) over our holes. Around the holes we dug ditches to provide for rain runoff. But we never expected what would happen in the next few days! A storm hit us with all of its fury.

The hill where we were situated became a slippery mess of oozing mud. The rain was so heavy it overflowed the ditches and flowed into our holes. The rain was unrelenting, as it beat down on our fortifications. To add to our predicament, the noise of the pelting rain made it impossible to see or hear anything beyond our perimeter.

We were in for more trouble than just the storm. The possibility of an enemy attack now became every man's concern. In the driving rain the Japanese could come within inches of our holes, and we would never know it. We would be defenseless, especially in the face of a grenade attack. It would be impossible to hear or detect any kind of movement. We were at the mercy of the enemy, and the storm.

My foxhole filled up with over a foot of water. It literally became a bathtub! Every inch of my body was wet, and the

One of our officers used to say, "The three 'F's of combat are fog, fatigue, and fear."

chilly night air added to my misery. One moment my feet would ache from the dampness, and the next moment I would have no feeling at all.

But the exciting thing about this experience is that during the daylight hours God gave me another portion of Scripture that was just what I needed for the night. It was Micah 7:8: "Do not gloat over me, my enemy! Though I have fallen, I will arise. Though I sit in darkness, the Lord will be my light." This along with that verse from Psalm 4:8 became my support and strength. That night I needed it.

It was the fourth night when someone thought we were being attacked. A single shot, and then another, alerted everyone. Guns blazed in the darkness. We were all shooting. It was a great emotional relief to be firing our rifles, even though we couldn't see anyone!

In the midst of this my rifle jammed, and I just about panicked! Here was my chance to avenge myself on the enemy, and my rifle wouldn't work!

I prayed for wisdom, calmness, and the ability to "see." In the darkness I was a blind man. Everything had to be by touch. I took out of my pocket a dirty rag, which I used for a handkerchief; spread it out between my legs on the muddy floor of my foxhole. I dismantled my rifle, laying the parts on the cloth. I found the problem quickly, and put it all back together again. I loaded the rifle, raised it straight up in the air, pulled the trigger, and the bullet went flying into the night. The Lord had helped me to do in the dark what I thought could only be done in the light.

For over a week I was wet night and day. But when I was off duty in the night watches, I slept! God had answered my prayer, and I thanked Him. Not only did I maintain my sanity, but the Lord also spared us from attack.

We never really understood why the Japanese did not attack. It was their chance to wipe us off the hill, but God in His mercy protected the whole company. I have often asked the Lord, "Did You spare our company because there was at least one praying man on the line?"

7

INTIMATE TALKS WITH GOD

Moving into hill country and up Highway 5, the fighting became very intense. We were losing so many men it began to look like we would all be gone in a matter of a few days. The normal size of a platoon at full strength was forty men. We were down to eight! Our company was at half strength—about one hundred men.

Even though casualties were heavy, it was a relief to keep fighting. We didn't have time to think about our losses, or to dwell on the horrible reality of the war. But when we stopped for any length of time, it gave me personally an opportunity to reflect and talk with God, which was more than just crying out to Him, "Help!"

With our casualty rate so high, I had a very strange and weird petition. I told the Lord how I wanted to die. I wasn't losing my faith or hope. I just wanted to make sure that God had heard me, and would grant me this one request.

This prayer came out of a growing anger and hatred for the Japanese because of the reports that were coming about

I do not subscribe to the maxim, "There are no athiests in foxholes,"
but I am sure that war can not rob a true believer of his faith in God.

ambushes and booby traps. I just wanted never to die under these circumstances. I think most soldiers shared my perspective—it would be OK to die, just so long as it happened while fighting. To die without a fight literally made me sick.

Surprise attacks were really something else. Men died without having a chance to fight back. At least I wanted to go down firing a shot, or throwing a hand grenade, or jabbing with a bayonet.

I remember praying: "Lord, it's OK if I die so long as my rifle is blazing. Yes, and I am content to die so long as the enemy is in my sights when I fire my last shot."

What prompted my prayer were two new kinds of terror tactics that became common in the battle zone. But this also raised my anger to a new level, and brought on a new degree of anxiety, not only for me but the others as well.

The enemy chose to pull back behind us and focus on harassing our supply route. We knew the Japanese were out there, but where? Almost every night in the foothills and mountains there was the possibility of a sneak attack. Also attacks began to increase during daylight hours as our supply lines grew longer. These attacks took place in areas where the terrain and the thick jungle made it easy for the Japanese to strike a quick blow, and then melt away into the jungle.

As we moved along Highway 5, we were constantly on patrol in order to keep our supply line open. This was done either on foot or in armored vehicles. But there was no way to guarantee that the road would be safe for any amount of time.

Along the road in the most unlikely places, the enemy chose to strike. For example: in one specific area the road was straight, and had only a few scattered trees on both sides. As usual the motorized patrol had come through, and declared the road safe and clear of any enemy.

Late that afternoon there was chilling news. The enemy had devised new kinds of tactics unheard of before. The Japanese had strung a heavy kind of wire—like piano wire—

across the road, tied around a large tree on either side. The target was the jeeps and their passengers, who were officers mainly. Usually the jeeps traveled with their windshields down, since the reflection of the sun on the glass could give away its position to the enemy. So men riding in the jeep would face into the wind.

The wire was carefully laid on the ground across the road so that the larger trucks could pass over it without difficulty. But when a jeep came along, they pulled the wire tight. This made it just high enough to clear the front of a jeep and low enough to catch the driver and its occupants under the chin.

One time a jeep carrying four men, traveling at a good speed along the straight portion of the road, hit a wire. Before anyone knew it, they were decapitated.

The other new incident was the booby-trapping of bodies—both dead Japanese and Americans alike. For our fallen comrades it would happen when one of them was killed, and we were unable to retrieve the body before nightfall. Under cover of darkness the Japanese would sneak out, anchor dynamite charges to the body, and then retreat.

In the morning, when our unsuspecting soldiers went out to recover the body, there would be a surprise explosion. The Japanese did this even with their own dead, since they had heard that American soldiers liked to search the Japanese for souvenirs! The action of moving the body would trip a detonator, which in turn would blow up those nearby leaving them badly wounded, maimed, or dead.

I prayed, "Lord, I am willing to die, but don't let it be like what I am hearing more and more about."

The high command took action. In a matter of hours a protective hook was devised to bolt onto the front end of all jeeps. This would catch and break any wire. It saved many lives.

Second, I took precautions, too. I stopped looking for souvenirs on the body of any enemy that had been left overnight.

But neither of the above decisions could help me with my anger toward the Japanese. I just let it boil inside. I had absolutely no remorse or guilt about killing them. I found myself praying that for every American who was killed in the fashion mentioned above, I would get three or four of them!

The author on the edge of one of his foxholes,
1954.

8

ENEMY OF A DIFFERENT KIND

What would take place after we moved from the low-level hills would become another kind of experience. We would face a new enemy—the mountains!

The terrain would compound our problems, and presented a challenge that would be almost as daunting as the Japanese. We would be looking up at steep, jagged formations that loomed ahead like great fortresses. Some of the peaks were over a mile high, with enemy artillery observation posts perched on top, where they could see our every move.

As we looked at our maps, we saw the major objective of Balete Pass outlined in red. It was obvious that from now on the battle would be uphill all the way, and that we would have to take the high ground if we were to win. No one talked about it, but we all knew in our hearts that it would be a bloody and costly campaign. The command was: "On and into the battle!"

The slopes were so steep in places that we were forced to literally claw our way up. As we inched our way along, physical exhaustion was a constant companion. Carrying our packs (about nine kilos or twenty pounds) along with our rifles, bay-onets, and ammunition (bullets and hand grenades) added to the burden.

The ridges narrowed in many places to as little as fifteen meters. These small plateaus would be protected by steep sides. In some situations, where there was exposed rock, a soldier could slip and find himself at the bottom of a hundred-meter ravine. Two or three enemy soldiers, strategically placed on a narrow ridge, could hold up our advance for days.

Add to this the thick jungle. It was like a great green fence to keep us at bay. We were doing as much hacking at the jungle as we were firing our rifles. Besides this there was frustration and anger because of the thick root systems that made digging a foxhole almost impossible.

In these situations our Filipino partners were there with their bolos (big-bladed native knives) to help hack paths through the tangled mass of vines. Faithfully and daily they exposed themselves to the enemy to keep the trails clear. It was costly. Many of them lost their lives as a result of enemy fire. But they never gave up regardless of the danger.

The undergrowth provided an excellent place for the enemy to hide. It gave them the advantage of being along the trail without being detected. This in turn set the stage for many an ambush—the ultimate terror for every soldier. The enemy could be within two meters of the trail, and not be detected.

Suddenly there would be a volley of shots, and our men would be cut down. By the time we recovered from the initial surprise attack, the enemy had melted back into the jungle.

On many a late afternoon we faced precarious situations. Once, the enemy cut off our supply line, isolating us from con-tact with our main body of troops. A typhoon prevented air-planes from dropping us supplies. The roaring storm blew away everything that we failed to tie down, and uprooted trees within the perimeter.

We never knew how long it would be before there was res-cue and help. This kind of setting put nerves on edge, and made

The slopes were so steep in places that we were forced to literally claw our way up.

us extra tense. Men were short-tempered and abrupt with each other. Every man's thoughts were on survival and supplies. *If there was an attack, would we have enough ammunition to hold out until reinforcements arrived?* There was terror, and lots of prayer!

Then one night it happened. We all thought we were under attack. Every man was alert, blazing away at an unseen foe. We were firing into the darkness, hopefully repulsing an invasion.

The firing continued sporadically for the duration of the darkness. In the morning there was a surprise—no enemy was found. Worst of all we had used up a good amount of our ammunition, which could spell trouble later on. There was no question about it. We were trigger-happy! But we were also at the mercy of the enemy.

Three days later friendly troops broke the blockade, and we were set free. But it took days to feel normal again. The trauma created by the possibility of no escape, and the prospect of running out of ammunition left a deep impression on all of us. I made a decision that from now on I would carry two extra bandoleers of bullets, no matter how heavy they felt.

As we came off the mountain for a hot meal and a brief rest, I was convinced of two things: God is in control and God intervenes.

Another lesson came as a result of those nights and days in isolation. If men think there is the slightest chance of getting out of a difficult situation, they will not pray. But if they think there is no way out, every man prays. Those few nights and days every man was praying because we all knew we didn't have a chance in the face of an attack. It was good for me personally to know that God was in charge, and He had intervened!

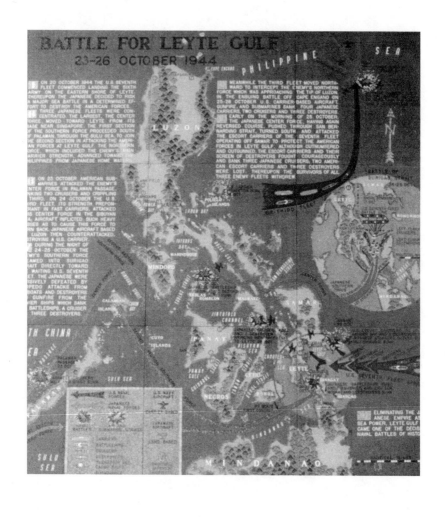

BATTLE FOR LEYTE GULF
23-26 OCTOBER 1944

9

CAPINTALAN RIDGE AND MAGGOT HILL

It was now time to press the attack on a hill. The configuration of the land looked like a closed fist with the index finger pointing straight out. The "finger" (Capintalan Ridge) was a small rise, attached to the "fist" or mountain (Maggot Hill).

This was only the beginning of the Japanese' mountain lines of defense. We did not realize at the time that we would face this same kind of fortification—ridge after ridge—with the enemy dug in, and committed to fighting to the finish with no surrender!

Even though our side mounted an intense artillery bombardment, there was no way to assess the damage, or to know how many of the enemy were dead. Later we learned that they simply retreated farther underground until the shelling was lifted. Then they would peek out through their bunkers and foxholes, waiting for us to advance. This meant two things: First, we had to expose ourselves time and time again. Second, the more exposure there was, the greater the number of casualties.

The Capintalan Ridge experience would be repeated over and over again. For two days we had waited as artillery pounded the hill and sent a great column of smoke and dust into the sky. The jungle that was on the slope of the "finger and the fist" had been reduced to piles of brush and kindling. The destruction of foliage gave us a good view of the defenses. But it also provided the Japanese with an excellent opportunity to see us advancing across the open territory. Besides their heavy small-arms fire, they would roll out their artillery pieces, fire at us at point-blank range, and then retreat back into the caves, taking their big guns with them.

The strategy for our infantry was simple: Try to get to the enemies' bunkers and foxholes before they realized the bombardment was over. The quicker we got there, the fewer casualties we had.

As we crouched and waited for the artillery to lift, we wondered whether any Japanese were still alive. The artillery stopped, and we advanced in a skirmish line, scrambling over pieces of brush, rocks, and debris to reach the fortifications immediately ahead.

Our timing was off! We were still about fifty meters away from their bunkers, when our artillery stopped. From a small foxhole, a Japanese popped up and pointed his pistol. But I was looking elsewhere. I caught a glimpse of him out of the corner of my eye, but it was so sudden that I had no time to swing my rifle around and fire. I was the only target directly in front of him.

Death flashed before me and in an instant I said, "Lord, I'm dead!" But at that moment a fellow soldier had caught the movement, and his rifle barked. He ended the Japanese's life and that saved mine. Once again, the Lord had spared me.

We continued to move up the hill, and past a line of small Japanese foxholes. All of us blasted away, keeping up a constant volley of bullets, and peppering the slits (narrow openings for observation and firing) of the bunkers. Our goal now was to get ourselves above the bunkers' slits. As some of the soldiers

It soon became evident that the whole ridge line was swarming with Japs, and bristling with automatic weapons.

continued a blanket of fire, the rest of us scrambled to the top safely and out of the line of fire from the Japanese. At this point, while we were now protected from enemy fire, the bullets from our fellow soldiers were coming in desperately close—just underneath where we were located. One slip or poor aim from a firing rifle could mean death from our own men.

We stopped to catch our breath, and to listen as our men stopped shooting. In that moment of a lull in the battle, we could hear Japanese voices from inside their bunkers.

Now our major objective was to get the enemy to surrender. Pamphlets had been provided, which were weighted with a piece of metal so they could be thrown easily. It stated in big letters written in Japanese: "SURRENDER: YOU ARE LOSING THE WAR. COME OUT, AND WE WILL SPARE YOUR LIVES."

I joined other soldiers in throwing the surrender leaflets into the openings. It was both difficult and dangerous. Lying flat on my stomach, I inched my way up and above the slit. By reaching down I could actually touch the top of the opening. But my position for throwing was very awkward.

From a prone position I reached down, and threw the surrender leaflet into the slit below. It worked!

We waited for what seemed like an eternity. We knew they had received and read the offer because of the excited talking we heard coming from within. We threw in a couple more surrender messages and waited. But we got no response. No one came out.

The command was given: "Seal the holes." I pulled the pin of a grenade, and threw it inside just like I had thrown the surrender leaflets. There was a belch of smoke from the explosion, and I could hear coughing. And then silence. I repeated the action, to make sure that the enemy was away from the opening so our sappers (dynamite experts) could throw in a charge that would destroy the bunker and seal it forever.

Our sappers brought up charges, and one by one the caves were sealed shut. They moved from opening to opening, and the same fate awaited the bunkers that dotted the mountain slope. There were no surrenders.

We reached the summit. But the Japanese were waiting from a higher ridge beyond. Some soldiers were decoyed to draw fire, and the enemy opened up with a blistering barrage. But it was a waste of ammunition on their side. We sustained no casualties, although we did have to keep our heads down.

On the other side of the ridge the Japanese were dug in for one final stand. They were dangerously close—within grenade-throwing distance. There was a warning of a possible *banzai* charge. Another company on our right flank had just experienced such an attack. This meant hand-to-hand combat. They were so many, and they came on so fast, it was impossible to shoot them all.

Our artillery observer, seated in a small plane that was circling our position, warned about the massing of troops on the Japanese side. Our only hope was to bring our own artillery in a location that was dangerously close to where we were located. But before this could be done we had to dig in. We were given thirty minutes. There was feverish activity as we tried to provide a shelter to protect ourselves from our own firepower. Then without further warning our mortars and artillery took over. We hugged the earth as shells flew over our heads and exploded, shaking the ground under us.

All the rounds cleared us. The closest ones hit the crest. The Japanese side of the ridge took a devastating pounding for the balance of the afternoon. When dusk came, the observer in the plane announced that he could see no movement on the enemy side.

Evening was coming. With the lingering daylight, we crawled out on our stomachs up to the crest of the bill, peeked over and waited. There was no movement, and we detected no life.

As darkness began to fall, and as there was no possibility that the enemy from the higher ground on the next ridge could see our movements, half of us began to dig in on the very top of

Hunger taught us that the living must eat under any circumstances.

our ridge. The other half of the men moved across the ridge to make sure that there were no survivors. Every body was checked out to make sure it was a dead one. There were scores of bodies and body parts littering the area. We had to push and drag bodies away to make room for our foxholes.

The next day as dawn was breaking the enemy opened fire, and we quickly moved out from our holes on the ridge and down on the backside, so that the gunners could not see us. This would be our daily procedure.

Within two days the bodies on the other side of the ridge began deteriorating. The stench was almost unbearable. The air was filled with putrid odor as the hot sun accelerated the decomposition. The smell was overpowering. Our food and drinking water began to taste like decaying flesh, making it difficult to either drink or eat.

The order was given to hold the hill at any cost, and we did. We named it "Maggot Hill." Ten days after the initial assault, we were relieved by another company, but the lingering impact of the smell of death stayed on with us for days. Amid the death and destruction of that assault, not one American was killed, and only a handful of the men had minor wounds. It was a miracle, to say the least.

In the midst of this carnage we had a surprise visitor. The chaplain, a godly man, had heard about the situation and came to give us encouragement. He invited those of us who were able to join him for a worship service of thanksgiving because our casualties were so minimal. The little pump organ that his Filipino assistant carried and played sent notes drifting into the air that lifted our spirits. He always played the favorite hymn of the troops, "The Old Rugged Cross."

There was a saying floating around: "There are no atheists in foxholes." That statement rang true then. Even the most callous men were willing to come, give thanks, and take communion. We all knew we had experienced a miracle.

10

ANOTHER RIDGE, ANOTHER DELIVERANCE

The struggle for each ridge had three things in common. First, death would always be there—especially for our troops, since as we advanced we had to expose ourselves to enemy fire. Second, the unexpected always would happen. Third, choices that seemed simple or insignificant could either save or destroy lives. But we would never knew the result of our choices until later. It would be this way that day as our platoon (we were down from forty-two to about twenty-five men) tried to take another high ground.

For several days we had tried to advance but to no avail. The enemy was dug in, and each assault previously tried had cost us men. The plan for today was changed. Rather than attacking from the lower end of the ridge, we would move around and try to take it from a different angle. Since infantry was too close to call in artillery, short-range mortars would be used to hit the ridge one more time. Then our platoon would attack.

As the mortar shells stopped, it became uneasily quiet. There was no enemy fire as we started scrambling up the hill. I was the number one man out in front, followed by the lieutenant, who in turn was followed by a second scout. Right away we were faced with heavy undergrowth that was tangled by previous shellings. So a choice had to be made—go over the top of the mounds of tangled bushes or go underneath. Hastily in a hushed tone the lieutenant said, "We'll go under." That decision kept us from being detected later, which in turn set us up for a miracle.

As quietly as possible, we were inching our way—crawling and sometimes just moving on our stomachs. There was no breeze, and the air was stifling hot. We stopped often to rest, catch our breath, and listen. It was deathly quiet. Once in a while there would be the snap of a twig, but we felt it was nothing out of the ordinary.

We reached a fallen tree that was near the summit of the ridge, and which lay parallel to our advance. The lieutenant was about a meter away from the trunk. I was on his left and about two meters away from him.

Lieut. Hicks whispered, "Stop moving, and listen. Look to the right. Do you see anything?"

Up until now I was so busy struggling to advance that I didn't notice anything. Then I looked. There to my right were trenches and two foxholes! Beyond that the brush was too thick to see clearly. The lieutenant and I both came to the same scary conclusion—we had penetrated the Japanese defense line!

We were literally lying between a string of enemy foxholes. Our position was very dangerous, and yet there was still no sign of the enemy. At this point in time I was thinking: *It's a trap!*

As I waited for a decision from Lieut. Hicks, I suddenly saw movement, and my heart started pounding. There on the other side of the log appeared the helmet of an enemy; then there was a face; then shoulders and then hands holding a rifle at the ready position.

I didn't dare move. It would give away my position. Besides there was no way that I could swing my rifle around because of the brush. I held my breath. I watched him as he surveyed the territory, and then disappeared.

I whispered to the lieutenant: "There's a Jap on the other side of the log!"

Lieut. Hicks quietly responded: "Lay still. He'll be back again." Then he rolled over on his back, shifted himself to where he could see the top of the log, and put his rifle into the ready position. We waited for what seemed like an eternity.

The silence of the morning was disturbed by movement and the crackling of tree twigs. In seconds the spy was back and looking again. At point-blank range the lieutenant pulled the trigger and blasted the lone figure. The shot blew him backward, and I am sure into eternity.

But it was a mistake! We should have retreated. Now the enemy knew where we were. I said, "Grenades!" We both knew that just one could spell death for us both!

The lieutenant urgently said, "Let's get out of here!"

Now the very brush that kept us from being discovered trapped us from escape. It was an agonizing time. We knew our lives were in the balance. But still there was no enemy action.

We did get away, and not one grenade was thrown at us nor one shot fired. God had spared us.

The next morning a new plan was devised because of what we had discovered. Another platoon was able to take the hill, but not without a battle. The troops blew up the network of holes and trenches, and cleared out the enemy.

A few days later, when I could write a letter home, I could not stop reflecting on God's faithfulness. The lieutenant, who had little respect for God, was one of those assigned to censor the mail. He and other officers of the company, plus the first sergeant, read every letter written by us men. It was their responsibility to check our mail, and cut out any thing that might yield valuable information to the enemy, and/or give away our position in the battle zone.

Lieut. Hicks knew I was a Christian. He had read too many of my letters to think otherwise. There were lots of things in them about the Bible and the Lord. (In the past, reports from home mentioned that many of my letters had been cut up.)

This time I described in detail what had happened, and he let my whole letter go through!

My father acknowledged that the letter had come without censorship! The lieutenant's action reflected just exactly what I felt and wrote—God had done something special for the two of us!

After this experience there was a new bond and warmth between the lieutenant and myself. We didn't talk about this incident, but both of us knew that God had spared our lives!

11

EXAMPLE OF FILIPINO COURAGE

I remember Rudy. He was typical of hundreds of Filipinos who had volunteered to help the Americans. He carried supplies to the front, and served as a stretcher-bearer for the wounded and the dead. Rudy's one great desire was to have a rifle.

On this day of battle, as usual, the stretcher-bearers were there for a call to action. Rudy had been waiting patiently all day, and now his time had come. Nick, a member of our squad (composed of ten to twelve men, see glossary), lay dying or dead about twenty-five meters away.

It was early afternoon. Our squad of eight men was advancing up a steep incline to gain a ridge when we came under heavy fire. Enemy snipers had moved into positions that threatened our whole squad. We were pinned down, and every time one of us tried to move we drew fire.

Our company commander and two squads of men were crouched behind a large fallen log, which provided relative safety and a good view of what was going on. From there the captain was shouting orders and directing the course of action. Men were moved into position behind the log, where they could hopefully sight the snipers, who were in a series of foxholes along the ridge.

Our men were quickly able to wipe out two snipers, which gave some relief to those of us under fire. But the intensity of enemy fire was still so great that the captain ordered us to retreat. Those of us out front began to slide down the hill on our stomachs to safety. It wasn't easy, and we did not dare so much as roll over, since the snipers were shooting at every movement we made.

I had been the lead man, so this meant that I would be the last one who would clear the hill. I was slithering on my stomach down and away when I realized that Nick had stopped.

Now my sergeant shouted: "Nick, be calm. Keep sliding down the hill. We'll give you a blanket of fire. Stay low. You'll be out of danger in about five yards."

Then it happened. Nick was prone, and then tried to roll over on his side. This move was just enough to expose part of his body. A shot rang out and hit him. The sergeant shouted: "Don't move. Stay flat!"

I looked and to my horror Nick sat up, and cried out in panic: "Don't you know I'm wounded. Mother, Mother!"

He started to struggle to his feet, which made him an easy target. The next bullet knocked him down.

As I continued my slide down the hill, the captain called: "Chuck, go back and check out Nick. Is he dead or alive?" This meant I had to start up the hill again, and expose myself to the same sniper that had shot Nick.

I prayed, *Lord, calm my heart, and help me get Nick.*

As I moved up the hill alongside a tree stump, the sniper shot at me three times. I could see on the stump where the bullets had hit—they were all at about the same level. The sniper could probably see only the top of my helmet. I figured that I would be safe so long as I stayed below the line of where the three shots had hit.

I called out to Nick but he didn't respond. I moved up to where I could touch his foot, reached out and grabbed it as the sniper shot again. I shook his leg but no response. I assumed he was dead.

The sergeant called out: "If he's dead, grab his BAR." (A Browning Automatic Rifle that fired like a machine gun.) I tried, but it was too dangerous to get the weapon. My every move drew fire. If I moved into position to get the automatic rifle, my head would be exposed. So I slid down the hill and began to move toward the log, behind which the captain was located.

The rest of the squad had run for safety, and now it was my turn. The captain shouted that they would lay down a blanket of fire, and when they did I should run for it. With the first volley of shots I was up and over the log, and safe.

It was about four o'clock in the afternoon, when the captain called me over for a briefing so that we could retrieve Nick—dead or alive—before nightfall. Rudy and another stretcher-bearer joined us to discuss the best way to approach Nick.

The two stretcher-bearers wore white armbands with red crosses tied around their arms, as per the Geneva Convention agreement. This was to signal to warring parties that these men were unarmed, and were on a mercy mission. According to international law, this agreement was to be respected. But we all knew from past experience that the Japanese would not honor this.

The plan was simple. We would lay down a blanket of fire in the direction of the snipers. Then Rudy and his partner were to jump over the log, go straight to where Nick was lying, pick up his body and return.

Rudy looked at me with a half smile, but I could see apprehension and fear. Nevertheless I knew he was determined from the few words we shared together. The two men told the captain, "We're ready." In a moment life could be over for them both.

Filipino carriers helped bring our dead down from the line while fighting raged in the mountains on either side of the valley.

Our men starting firing, and Rudy rose up, to take the lead. In the din and roar of the firing rifles no one heard the Jap's shot. Rudy straightened up, his body shuddered, and he fell to the ground at my side. He was dead. The enemy had ignored his armband.

He had waited all day for this opportunity, and his only reward was death. He deserved a medal. He never got the rifle he longed to have, but he died with great honor with a stretcher in his hand.

Nick's body wasn't recovered until the next day. When we finally got to him, we found his body had been stripped, and his automatic rifle missing. It gave me an eerie feeling to think that the enemy could turn our own weapon on us sometime in the near future!

12

EVERY CHOICE A CRISIS

There is a saying that lieutenants, like scouts, have a very short life span—in combat their average life is about one week. The reason for this is that when advancing the lieutenant is the first man out after the scouts—he leads the platoon. In some situations the lieutenant would have to join the scouts in order to assess the situation. His very movement would attract a sharpshooter's bullet. (Also, on the battlefield lieutenants could be identified by their lightweight rifle called a carbine, which was smaller in size than what a regular foot soldier carried.)

There had been no contact for three days. We were moving up the Old Santa Fe Trail when a burst of machine-gun fire disturbed the tranquility of the beautiful morning, and threw our patrol into confusion.

The little valley had been burned off the day before so there was no place to take cover. On the scorched ground not even a blade of grass was available to hide behind.

A shout: "Medic (first-aid man) forward!" spelled trouble. Several were wounded and in desperate need of care. The medic

We continued to receive artillery from Bolong, Sta. Fe, and the Villa Verde Trail although we now held the dominating terrain all along the line.

moved forward to give assistance. Then a message was relayed to those of us in the rear: "Lieut. Hicks is dead; Sgt. Springer is now in command of the platoon."

An order was shouted to take cover, but the nearest rocks and a tree were about twenty-five meters away. That horrible urge to run gripped me. I wanted to get up and get out of there. But to do this would mean certain death. It was a frightening choice.

Choices can cause agony and even regret. They can bring a smile to one's face, or terror to one's heart. In most instances there is no time to think. If a soldier can't make a choice, someone else will make it for him. In some situations every step, every move, every minute, every second can mean life or death for you, or for someone else. On the front line no one has the luxury of living a day at a time, especially when a second can seem like an eternity.

It was not my turn to be point man, so I was back at the rear of the column of the platoon. After my first reaction to run, there was a sense of relief, since the firefight was well ahead of me. But things quickly turned to be dangerous for all of us. The enemy knew exactly where we were, and began to drop mortar shells in our direction. I could hear them exploding behind me, with each explosion coming closer.

I prayed, as I had done on more than one occasion, *Lord, do I just stay here or run for those rocks?* It seemed that either place could eventually mean death. The bullets were flying over our heads as mortar shells were coming in on us from the rear.

Some men ran for the rocks, and made it. Others just stayed in place on their stomachs. My choice was to stay where I was—flat on the ground.

The enemy shells were creeping up. The first one exploded about one hundred meters away; the next one was about eighty meters; the next about sixty meters. As I heard the explosions come nearer and louder, I knew that eternity could be just minutes away.

My heart was pounding, as I sensed death approaching. It was a strange feeling—I was afraid but I wasn't afraid, as I told the Lord I was ready to come home.

You cannot realized the cost of war, until you start collecting your own dead.

The next two shells came in, but to our surprise those two shells were duds! They landed but didn't explode. A third shell came in very close, but again it was a dud! And then no more shells. Once again the Lord had me in the right place at the right time! In my nerve-shattered condition, as we were rescued, I breathed a prayer, "Thank You, Lord."

The wounded and the dead had been accounted for—the dead were bagged, and the wounded were readied for evacuation. And now it was time to move men up in rank. I thought it was my time for advancement. But the first sergeant had other plans because he had friends. Two other men, Williams and Frank, were promoted to Staff Sergeant/squad leader and Buck Sergeant/assistant squad leader instead of me.

In late afternoon we dug our foxholes at specific places assigned by the first sergeant. Frank and Williams were placed at the ends of the squad to dig in, since they were now in positions of leadership. The remaining seven men in the squad were given assignments between these two men. That night I bedded down in my hole with anger and disgust at the first sergeant—and I was blaming God, too.

After all, I had seniority!

In the middle of the night the silence was shattered by the explosion of enemy mortar fire. The attack was sudden and over very quickly. All of us were immediately covered with dust and the smell of exploding shells. This is when soldiers feel frustrated—the enemy had attacked, but we had no one to shoot at! After the initial shells had crashed and exploded, there was silence for a moment, and then cries of anguish and pain from those who were wounded.

In the morning I learned that Frank, the man who had been promoted to Buck Sergeant and assistant squad leader before me, had his arm blown off. For all intents and purposes, I should have been in his foxhole. But now I was to be moved up. My rank now was Buck Sergeant, and my position was second in command, which meant I would bring up the rear of the squad rather than being the one out in front. My days as a scout were over.

The assignment for the day was to attack a series of bunkers that anchored a Japanese defense line. Williams, now Staff Sergeant although with less seniority, was now to lead the attack. It should have been my turn to lead. But no, once again it would be my time to wait.

The two scouts were sent out ahead with Sgt. Williams immediately following them. Within minutes there was heavy rifle and cannon fire and a raging battle. Sgt. Williams was blown into eternity.

Above the din of the battle, the captain shouted:

"Holsinger, move up and take charge!" In less than twelve hours I had moved from Private First Class to Staff Sergeant. God knew where he wanted me to be and when.

13

MORAN—
SHORT-TERM PARTNER

Moran stepping into my life was a jolt—a surprise! It wasn't so much who he was, but rather what he did that impacted me. Over the years his actions would bring back far reaching memories, and would teach me the meaning of what Jesus said on the cross: "Father, forgive them, for they do not know what they are doing" (Luke 23: 34). That word *forgive* would take on new significance for me in the next five days, and would stick with me for the rest of my life...

Moran was a "new" soldier, taking the place of someone who had been wounded or killed. On the first four days that a replacement joins the company he is not immediately put in the front line. Rather he digs his hole in the middle of the perimeter, along with the captain, company headquarters personnel, and the mortar platoon. This is done so that when he finally joins the front line he will be accustomed to the sounds of night, and hopefully will not panic in the darkness. When in the middle of the perimeter, the instructions are very explicit—do not shoot. Any movement inside the perimeter is our own men. Don't panic!

On many occasions, the company would not be on the move, which was a great relief. It would mean that we would have two or more days before digging again. Also, if the ground was exceptionally hard and/or the setting called for it because of the terrain, we would dig in on the "buddy system," two men to a hole. Under the "buddy system" I would eventually meet Moran.

In the middle of the third night, Moran woke up, heard noises, and in the moonlight saw movement—someone was crawling. He panicked, grabbed his rifle, and fired one shot. He killed Sgt. Cotton, who was simply on his way to wake up the next man for guard duty.

Cotton was my squad leader, since the days of Guadalcanal. But more than that he was a very special friend. We enjoyed talking about home and family. His mother had encouraged him to join the peacetime army because she felt he needed the discipline. At times we talked about spiritual things, and I shared with him what it meant to be a Christian. He knew a lot of the answers because he had gone to Sunday School in a little town in Colorado.

Cotton was a tough-seasoned career soldier. He could curse and swear like the rest of the men, but he also had a soft and warm side to him. When we were in New Caledonia, several times we went to town together. I never drank, but he wanted me along to make sure that if he got drunk, he would get back to camp without getting into trouble. He was an excellent soldier and mentor.

It was on Vella Lavella, an island in the Northern Solomons, that we shared a hole under the "buddy system." This was where I learned to keep alive and alert. While recognizing God's protection of me, at the same time it was providential that I ended up in the same foxhole with Cotton. I survived on more than one occasion because of what this "old" soldier had taught me.

Cotton had often said with a curse when he was either sober or drunk: "The Japs will never get me. If I die it will be at the hands of my own blankety-blank men!" He said this half-jokingly, both in disdain for the Japanese, and because he knew his men appreciated him. Unfortunately, his prophecy had become reality.

The crushing blow for me was that this new guy—whoever he was—had killed a special friend. I didn't want to see Moran, let alone talk to him!

It was now time for Moran to be assigned to the front line, and much to my shock, the first sergeant put this man in my squad with me under the "buddy system!" I was furious. In my heart I couldn't understand why God would allow this to happen. Here was a man who to me was almost as bad as the enemy—after all, he had killed my friend!

My responsibility would be to help him become a good soldier. But I knew that if I did not forgive him, I wouldn't even talk with him. I also knew that training him could be crucial to both his and my survival. Maybe in the next battle we would desperately need each other. I quietly prayed, as Jesus did on the cross, "Father, I forgive him…" and I had immediate peace, but this didn't help the situation or heal my feelings. So for the first two hours, we hardly spoke. I couldn't hide my anger. He knew that every man in the line knew what he had done, and that they felt the same way as I did. The tension between us was indescribable.

Moran finally broke the silence…

In the midst of a war fighting is not constant. Exploding shells and the crackle of gun fire often fade out altogether. Often it can be days before a shot is fired. It is at times like this that a soldier gathers his thoughts. There are also quiet talks about home, family, and the old haunts. And if a soldier has left a girlfriend behind, it isn't long before the talk shifts to her. Then out come the pictures.

This was true with Moran. He fit the pattern. He broke the silence by asking me if I would take a look at his girlfriend's picture.

I said, "Sure." This melted the ice, and we were talking.

Now one subject that soldiers considered taboo to talk about was death. The general attitude is that death will be for the other guy, but not for me. But there is no question about it, the thought of death hung heavy over each one of us. And the question always lingered: *Will I ever get home?* But Moran broke the mold on this one. He wanted to talk about death—his death!

I said, "Moran, before we get on that subject we need to talk about the war." And for the next three or four hours, I mentored Moran just like Cotton had mentored me. I figured that we would have a number of days to do this, but I was eager to get started so he would be ready for the night.

He would need to be taught about the finer points of the front line—the jungle, nighttime alertness, and survival. He would learn about distinguishing noises, when to shoot and when not to shoot his rifle, to be aware that the enemy will try to "bait" soldiers at night—have them fire—so as to give away their position, how to "see" at night and determine whether things are really moving or not, etc. If there is any doubt, wake me up. We would probably shoot, and then ask questions in the morning.

I told him how one time we thought we were being attacked, and there was a blaze of gunfire. The next morning we discovered that we had killed a carabao, which had wandered too close for comfort. We had a good laugh over this.

We ended up talking all day, and when night fell we were still talking in hushed tones. We stayed awake through each other's one and one half hours of guard duty.

A patrol had gone out the next morning, but had found no enemy. I was about to fall asleep, but Moran was writing. Suddenly he blurted out, "Chuck, here is a letter to my girlfriend. You gotta read it!" The letter startled me. In it he was writing about death. He felt that he didn't have long to live, and wanted to make sure that this letter was sent to his girlfriend. The letter went on talking about his soldiering in general, and life in the front line in particular—but he never mentioned the

The scouts came to a suspicious area. Two men were given specific instructions, and sent off the trail to each side... The lead scout saw movement to one side, which was way beyond where the wing man should have been. A head peeked around a tree. He saw the movement, whirled with his rifle and, firing from the hip, hit his target between the eyes.

man he killed. He wanted his girl to know that he loved her. He wrote in conclusion: "I sense that it won't be long before I am dead. I was a good soldier, and you would have been proud of me. I wish that I could kiss you one more time, but this letter will have to do it. Good-bye."

He turned to me, looked me straight in the eye, and said, "Chuck, you can't deny a fallen comrade. Swear to me that you'll send my letter."

I was at a loss for words. Finally I responded: "Don't talk this way. Don't even think like this! The odds are in your favor. Three out of five guys come through alive. One out of the last two will be killed. Sure, you might be wounded, but your chances are good."

We discussed the issue for a few more minutes. He insisted that I take the letter, and reluctantly I put it into my pack. The conversation had ended when word was passed along that there would be a hot meal from the field kitchen. We grabbed our mess kits and were on our way to supper.

The next day a patrol was sent out, which was a combination of two squads. I didn't have to go, but as squad leader, I sent Moran and one other man so as to have a twelve-man patrol. This would be his "baptism" in no-man's land. The patrol didn't encounter any enemy, and returned about two hours later. But there was no Moran!

At the debriefing it was explained that the scouts came to a suspicious area. Two men were given specific instructions, and sent off the trail to each side to make sure that the patrol would not be ambushed. Moran was one of those men. He went to the right. The lead scout knew where the two "wing men" were located before he moved out.

The scouts went forward, but as they returned, Brad, the front scout, who was a squirrel hunter from Tennessee and an excellent shot, saw movement to one side, which was way beyond where the wing man should have been. A head peeked around a tree. Brad saw the movement, whirled with his rifle and, firing from the hip, hit his target between the eyes.

It was Moran, who had moved beyond his original assignment, and exposed himself when he peeked around a tree. The patrol carried Moran's body back to the perimeter.

I was sick at heart. I went back to my foxhole and packed Moran's things so they could be taken along with his body. I wrote a quick PS on the envelope to his girlfriend: "Your boyfriend was killed today. He was on patrol, and died in the line of duty!" I couldn't write any more.

I sank into my foxhole overcome with agony and sorrow. I needed to cry, but I couldn't. I called out to God to give me tears, but they would not flow, and I wondered whether I would ever cry again.

The letter was sent, but I never did hear back from the girl.

14

THE WAR BEHIND ME

The war finally ended. I eagerly looked forward to going home. It was exciting and exhilarating when I finally touched the ground in the good old USA. I eagerly looked forward to finishing college, and to a career as an athletic coach.

As I stepped on the dock in Seattle, Washington, I was ecstatic. In my grand scheme of things I was quick to tell God what I thought was best for me and His Kingdom. I knelt down, kissed the ground and remembered praying, *If it is all right with You, Lord, I never want to leave the States again.*

I was long on asking God for everything—food, strength, protection—but I forgot the most important prayer of all: "…Thy will be done on earth as it is in heaven." God had other plans for me, one of which was to return to the Philippines—the last place on earth that I would choose to go!

From my earliest childhood I was interested in sports. Then as I grew older, I developed an interest in the Bible also, and in working with young people. There was always a feeling in the depth of my being that someday I would be able to use sports and the Bible together to reach young people for the Lord.

In my last year of high school I had read a story about a man who went to Libya (northern Africa) as a missionary with the YMCA. He invested his life in the young people teaching baseball and Bible to the youth of that country. He trained coworkers, and had over one hundred teams that competed against one another. Each practice and each game was preceded by Bible study and prayer.

After twenty-five years he retired. He had impacted a whole generation! Because of this the Libyan government decorated him with the highest medal that could be given to a civilian.

This man became my model. Someday and in some way I prayed that I would be involved in a similar way in sports.

15

CHALLENGE— RETURN TO THE BATTLE SCENE

I went back to Wheaton to finish college where the biggest excitement was meeting my life partner!

Elisabeth (Betty) Hermansen and I first met in a class by accident. The professor seated us students in alphabetical order, and so we were next to each other, our names both beginning with "H." (But I had earlier noticed Betty when she worked in the school cafeteria serving food. She always had a bright smile and a cheerful greeting for everyone, including me.) I asked her several times for a date, but I was always too late—she had already been asked out. Finally she invited me to her dorm party—and this was the beginning of our romance. The major thing that drew us together, other than our love, was our commitment to the Lord and missions. But we never dreamed that our call to missions would come like it did!

After I finished my college education, my first job was coaching at Wheaton College in Wheaton, Illinois. At the same time I was active in youth programs in high schools and in a

Betty and me. 1990.

With our two young children. Manila, 1955.

local church. My involvement in athletics gave me an opening into the lives of many students. I was excited because I could begin to see the fulfillment of a dream.

I had been following my dream for four years when my wife and I were confronted with a challenge on Easter Sunday, 1953 that would change the direction of our lives forever!

Back in 1951 Dr. Dick Hillis, a long-time missionary who had escaped from the Communists in China, went to Taiwan to minister to the army of Nationalist China. He responded to an invitation to share the Gospel with these soldiers, but the commanding general demanded more than that. He wanted entertainment and a morale-lifter for his troops. Out of this challenge came the concept of bringing a Christian basketball team to inspire and entertain the troops. It was good, solid, exciting entertainment, and the soldiers loved it.

But the team's main purpose was sharing the Gospel with the soldiers. This was done at halftime with the players giving testimonies, singing Gospel songs, and inviting the men to give their hearts to Christ. This was the beginning of Venture for Victory, which continues on to this day as Sports Ambassadors.

From Taiwan the news of the success of that Christian basketball team spread quickly and reached the Philippine Basketball Federation. And so before long there was an invitation: "Come over and help us! We need the same kind of entertainment for our people." The next year there was great enthusiasm in Manila, as the first team of many in years to come would invade the Philippines!

Betty and I will never forget the challenge from Dick Hillis, as he told us how excited the Filipinos were about basketball. Then he said, "Chuck, the Philippines needs coaches like you. There are at least a hundred men who would gladly take your place at Wheaton College, but it would be difficult to find even one man to go to the Philippines."

As we could not respond immediately there was a long period of silence. After a few moments, he then said thoughtfully, "Besides, your war experiences can be an open door to the hearts of the Filipinos."

Betty and I accepted the challenge. But then my nightmares began. War dreams that had almost vanished from my sleep were coming back like a flood. The dreams were a repeat performance every night—the face of the enemy was always the same! I would be struggling up a hill to destroy my Japanese opponent, then awaken before I could reach him. Or I would be running across a field with a Japanese plane overhead. I could see the pilot's wicked smile. Then my feet would get stuck, and at that moment he would drop a bomb. Just before it hit me, I would wake up in a cold sweat. There would be no sleep for the rest of the night.

After several weeks, I thought I would go crazy. Without sleep I realized that I could not go back to the Philippines hounded nightly by this kind of terror.

I told the Lord: "I cannot go!"

At this point in time my brother "Hap," who had become a missionary to China, and who was put under house arrest by the Communists, understood my plight. He came to my aid.

He said, "Tell me your dreams."

After hearing these in detail, he said: "Chuck, all your dreams have you on the defensive. Take the offensive. Let's look up verses in the Bible that will chase away the nightly terror."

We spent many days studying what the Bible says about fear. At the same time I began memorizing Bible verses like Psalm 27:1, "The Lord is my light and my salvation—whom shall I fear?" Psalm 56:3,4, "When I am afraid, I will trust in You. In God… I trust; I will not be afraid" And 2 Timothy 1:7, "God did not give us a spirit of timidity, but a spirit of power, of love, and of self-discipline."

With these words guarding my sleep, the Lord delivered me from my nightly anguish, and I was on my way back to the Philippines—the very place I said I never wanted to go again!

My brother Hap (he's a cowboy at heart) and me.

My family: Laura (who wrote me every week), me and wife Betty, sister-in-law Maura and brother Paul, Mother Elsie and Dad Paul, Dorothy and David.

16

EXCITEMENT IN MINISTRY

OUR FIRST TERM

We arrived in Manila on September 23, 1953 in the middle of a typhoon. What a reception! The wind blew so furiously it was almost impossible for the captain to get our ship secured at the pier. After three tries, we made it and were finally able to go ashore. But what flooding as we drove to our new home! However, our driver assured us that by noon the water would be gone. He was right. And it was just good to be in the place we knew God had chosen us to serve.

Early on in our first year we were visited by our Associate General Director. It was November, 1953. He had come to talk with us about long-term service, since our commitment then was only for a year. From oral and written reports of our work he recognized our effectiveness with young people. There were teeming numbers of youth that were open to the Gospel, so he asked us to consider a long term commitment.

I will never forget his words: "Chuck, are you and Betty willing to commit the rest of your lives to ministry in this country?"

What? But that night, Betty and I prayed earnestly about this, and the next morning we gave him our answer: "Yes!"

We were excited about the prospects of a long and satisfying career—learning the language and settling into using sports as a means of reaching young people for Christ.

The name of our organization in the country at that time was "Philippine Youth Crusades." It was a perfect description of what I was doing, and what others would do who would follow me. There would be basketball players, who would play against the semipro teams in Manila, hold basketball coaching clinics, and be involved in games in the provinces where they would share the Gospel at halftime. But for now and the next few months I would be the only one in this ministry.

The challenge of this country, which was struggling to emerge from the trauma and devastation of war, stirred both our hearts. We were excited about the future. We wanted to be partners with this nation and this people for a long time.

COME AND HEAR GEN. MACARTHUR'S SOLDIER!

I launched into the ministry with great enthusiasm. There were invitations from across the country to hold coaching clinics and to speak at school assemblies. On the main island of Luzon I traveled with a van that was equipped with loud speakers, a 16mm motion picture projector, a generator and a big two-way screen (measuring about four x six meters).

Nightly the big attraction in the plaza (town square) was a Billy Graham movie, which was a part of my presentation.

My daily schedule was to arrive in a village or town early in the day. There would be an assembly where I'd talk to the young people. (When the principals of the schools learned that I was a member of Gen. MacArthur's liberation forces, they would ask me to talk about the war.) After school there would be a coaching clinic on basketball. This would be followed in the evening with an evangelistic meeting in the town plaza in cooperation with the local pastors. After the Billy Graham film, I would climb to the platform on top of the van, give my testimony about my life and my war experiences, and top it off with a Bible message.

Every meeting people were responding to the invitation to accept Christ as their Savior and Lord. We would sign up those who responded for a free Bible correspondence course. After the evening meeting people would linger around, more to shake my hand because I had been with the liberation forces than for any other reason. It was evident that my war experiences were a key factor in gaining a receptive ear from the people.

THREATS AGAINST MY LIFE!

Almost immediately after World War II, growing numbers of dissident groups threatened the nation and the government. The two major ones that I knew about were the Communist Party (Maoist) and the local Huks. This latter group at one time had been friendly toward both the Americans and the Philippine government. But as the years went by, these groups became more and more impatient with the constitutional government until their impatience turned to disillusionment.

The United States (and Americans) were generally blamed, along with the Philippine government, for the nation's problems. Lawlessness was rampant, and anarchy was evident in many areas of the land.

In late 1953 the Communists and the Huks had taken over parts of Manila. It was a very tense time for every one—Filipinos and the American missionaries alike.

As I went out to the provinces, I was warned to stay away from certain areas because I was an American. The fear was real, but I didn't want to be motivated by fear. This caused a dilemma—should I go or not go?

I made the decision that I would not turn down any invitation. At the same time I prepared a miniature copy of my army discharge papers, and put it with my passport that I always carried with me. This would be evidence to Communists and/or Huks that I had fought for their country, and I had earned the right to be left alone.

There were times of tension when a pastor and/or a town official would warn me. On more than one occasion I was told: "We will try to protect you as much as possible, but we cannot guarantee your safety!"

One time in Ozamis City, in the southern island of Mindanao, I was asked to go and share nightly in the plaza. After I arrived there, word came that dissidents were going to kill me at the first night of meeting.

My host spirited me away, out the back window of his home, and took me on a four-hour walk into the bush to hide me from harm. We were met by two tough-looking men, who had the famous long-bladed bolo knives tucked in their waistbands.

My host said, "These men will take care of you." And I thought it meant my death! I must have shown fear in my face because my host quickly assured me: "These are your brothers. They are Christians. You do not have to be afraid."

After a day and a half, the danger passed. I returned, and had the joy of sharing for the remaining two days. The Lord gave us a great time, and a church was established because of this effort.

In the Bicol region near Legaspi City, there was a threat that turned into reality. A local group of people tried to disturb our meetings. They were chanting and making noise to negate what was being said, but our PA system overwhelmed their opposition.

The people tolerated the film, but in the middle of my talk they hit our vehicle. My interpreter frantically shouted, "We're being stoned!" Rocks were flying by our heads and against the side of the van. We leaped off the platform and sought cover inside the van. We stayed flat on our stomachs until after midnight, when we were rescued by a group of believers and the town mayor. Fortunately, no one was injured and damage to our equipment was minimal. But our attackers had smeared the van with human excrement.

I firmly believe that when the attackers learned that I had been with the liberation forces, they left me alone! Just as the Lord protected me during the war, He was looking after me then, as I went from school to school, and village to village.

The Lord had fitted and equipped me in and through my war experiences. As I reflected on all that I was doing, I realized that I was "prepared and protected" for a specific work. This made me dream of great days ahead!

POLITICAL STABILITY 1954

Late in 1953 the political situation, especially in Manila, was ripe for revolution. Into this picture stepped a "savior"! It was election time, and the people chose a man named Ramon Magsaysay to be their president. He was a World War II soldier who went after the rebel groups with his military leadership. His gallant efforts were very effective in cleaning up Manila, and in creating confidence in both the local and foreign communities.

He encouraged missionary activity and was a genuine friend, especially to those of us who had fought on Philippine soil. His commitment to provide a climate of peace gave me new assurance, as I went out into the provinces.

The tragedy is that at the midterm of his office he was killed in a plane crash in the southern part of the country. It was a shocking loss for all of us because he was on the side of the people and the missionaries.

17

REVISITING WAR AREAS

JANUARY 1954

An invitation had come for me to speak at the Annual Conference of the Methodist Church in the Philippines. This included the Caraballo Mountains and Southern Cagayan Valley Districts of Luzon. This visit would bring memories of the war back to me in living color.

Our journey along Highway 5 followed the general path that the Twenty-fifth Division took in retaking this territory from the Japanese. It goes through the Caraballo Mountains, over Balete (Dalton) Pass, and into the Cagayan Valley.

This would be a treat, because it would be an occasion for me to take along Betty as I relived this war chapter of my life. And it would be one more reminder of God's great faithfulness. The plus factor would be the opportunity to minister to the people living in this area of the country.

The rains stopped in mid-December, and this set the stage for our journey north in January. The time would also coincide with the army activities that took place in 1945.

We drove the "Glory Wagon" so named because of its utility as a conveyor of the Gospel. (See previous chapter regarding this van.) Our travel went north from Manila through two cities—Cabanatuan and San Jose—and the province of Nueva Ecija. The Battle for Lupao, which cleared the Central Luzon plain (mentioned in an earlier chapter), took place about thirty kilometers (twenty miles) to the west of San Jose. I relived the scene with Betty…

After Lupao we had only sporadic and minor encounters with the enemy. For about two weeks none of us in our company fired a shot. We were looking for and expecting the enemy, but he was no place to be found. It was about thirty kilometers north of San Jose that our army unit began to encounter resistance again.

Betty and I came to a small flat area by the roadside where it seemed like there was nothing. It was isolated and barren with no villages in sight. But this was a significant place for me. We climbed out of the wagon, and surveyed the territory. As the wind gently blew across the arid landscape, once more I could feel the tension and the anxiety of the war. I described the scene to Betty…

We dug in for the night, and would jump off in the morning heading toward Puncan, a small dot on the map. I would be the lead scout. Everyone was up, packed, and ready to go by 6:00 A.M. The two of us who would be the scouts moved forward to join Col. Larson and two Filipino guerrillas. We two point men—another name for the scouts—were given a briefing. On the map the guerrillas pointed out suspicious looking stony and wooded areas, which could be occupied by the enemy. It would be our responsibility to check these out. The guerrillas also reported that there was enemy activity the night before, and that it looked like they were laying land mines along the road. This news meant that any step could mean we'd be maimed or killed.

The colonel said that since there was the prospect of the enemy nearby, one of us was to maintain hand-signal contact

The 35th Infantry began a long end run...

...through a town called Carrangalan to attack Puncan and Digdig from the east.

with him as we advanced. We were to move out about two hundred meters in front of the main body—two hundred meters is a long way to be separated from help! This would be the greatest distance of separation between me and friendly troops as a scout that I would experience during the war.

The colonel continued: "Just keep moving until you discover the enemy, or they fire at you. Be alert for signals to stop or continue on."

The colonel's last words of instruction were sobering: "Heads up and success, soldiers. Remember the whole army is behind you." At that moment I felt sick in my stomach, and lonely in my heart. It was a soldier's dilemma—the fear of the unknown, and the possibility of dying alone in enemy hands.

The uncertainty of what was ahead at every turn in the road and the expectation of ambush, which was a constant terror, gripped me. Added to this was the prospect of land mines. Two hundred meters—the length of two soccer fields—could mean death with no hope of rescue.

The colonel asked, "Do you understand?" My legs were like rubber; I was too shaken to speak; I just nodded my head. For a nineteen-year-old boy, this was the hour when I had to grow up, and fast.

It was time to move out with my partner, Henry, who would be about twenty meters behind. I was overwhelmed by the thought that I would be the first soldier out in front of the whole army. It was anything but a prestigious position! This realization added to the burden of my responsibility.

I had read my Bible, and committed the day to the Lord about an hour before. Now there was only enough time to offer a prayer. I breathed, "Help, Lord!" In that moment I sensed the Lord's presence. There was horrendous fear, but I knew that whether I lived or died, I belonged to the Lord. I jumped to my feet; the Lord gave strength to my legs—I was on my way.

I decided to stay off the center of the road, and at the same time looked for freshly-turned soil, which could mean a buried land mine.

The cut of the road followed the contour of the hills, which made it almost impossible for us to maintain contact with our troops. Sometimes we cut corners—we'd be on the road, and then at other times scrambling over rough terrain and grass that was six feet tall. Our heads would bob up and down above the tall grass like swimmers in the sea. We were in trouble. We could not maintain contact as the colonel had ordered.

Now it was time to use our own initiative. Our choice was to keep moving ahead. Approximately three hours into our advance we came to a park-like area with heavy foliage and found the remains of a campsite. We could actually smell the enemy! (We could never figure it out, but there was a certain smell that the Japanese left at any place they stayed.) Cautiously searching the area, we found empty food ration cans. They were still moist. We figured that they had been opened that morning! In the soft dirt areas we found footprints and other fresh signs of activity.

Then my heart leaped into my throat. There in front of me were bloody bandages! As a scout, discovering things like these was very important, but it also caused anxiety and apprehension. The bloody rags were still wet!

In the silence of the morning, I wondered if we were being watched. It was agonizing to wait—looking, and expecting a shot to be fired. One thing for sure, we knew that the enemy was not too far away. The realization came to us that it would be just a matter of time before there would be contact, and a firefight.

By hand signals, the colonel knew we were onto something and called for our advance to stop. The main body of troops caught up with us and conducted a thorough search of the area. Providentially, for Henry and me, this delayed our advance for a couple of hours.

It was time for lunch break. My stomach was so tight I couldn't eat or drink. The tension of the morning had not subsided, and there was no chance to relax. But I was still alive. Nobody had shot at me, and I didn't fire a shot. And the colonel said that we had done a good job. I thanked the Lord!

As we prepared to jump off in the afternoon, Henry and I briefly talked about the empty ration cans, and the rags with sticky blood. One thing for sure, this evidence increased both our tension and alertness.

I asked myself: *Where is the enemy, and how will they strike?* I could see this question in Henry's face, too, and I knew he saw it in mine. I really thought that we were headed for an ambush, and my last afternoon on earth was about to begin.

We moved ahead for about five kilometers (approximately three miles), and came to a small group of deserted huts and houses. This was our objective for the day. It was midafternoon, and we had arrived at the outskirts of Puncan. There had been no contact with the enemy. But rather than chancing an encounter late in the day, it was decided that we had gone far enough.

It was now about 4:30 P.M., time to dig in for the night. But before Henry and I could start digging and settling in, we had to give a debriefing to our officers. As we moved along in the afternoon, we found discarded equipment and papers with Japanese writing. Henry and I made mental notes of the equipment. We gathered up the papers and turned them over to our intelligence officers—both were Japanese, only one was American-born. He read the papers. The intelligence officers looked at the evidence and determined two things: first, we were chasing ragtag elements of the enemy, which were retreating fast. Second, these enemy stragglers were on their way to join a larger unit.

The next morning another company took the lead, and our company moved to the rear as a reserve unit. It was just a few minutes after 7:00 A.M. when the lead company came under attack. The sound of automatic rifle fire broke the silence. Bullets were flying as we scrambled for cover.

The enemy was waiting for us at the other side of the village and inflicted severe casualties. (We later learned that the two scouts died instantly.) The battle lasted for two days, and we didn't move an inch forward after that. Because of heavy casualties, the decision was made to withdraw. A new strategy was being planned by the higher command, so we abandoned any hope of capturing Puncan.

Once again the Lord had protected me; I was not the advance man at a critical time. The timing of the delay at lunchtime saved Henry and me from certain destruction. (Our outfit, attacking from the north, took the village about four weeks later. This area became the temporary command post for our regiment.) That evening in the twilight, I opened my New Testament that included the Psalms and continued to work on memorizing Psalm 91. Especially meaningful was the second verse: "I will say of the Lord, He is my refuge and my fortress, my God, in whom I trust..."

In Puncan Betty and I looked for the remains of foxholes, but there were none to be found. Any diggings and signs of foxholes had eroded away over the past eight years. There were just too many rebuilding activities done in the village to see any remains of the war.

With great puzzlement, the local folks watched as I searched the surrounding land. It became clear to them when I introduced myself as a member of Gen. MacArthur's liberation forces, and showed them the general area where I had dug my foxhole. This caused great excitement. When they learned that I had actually been there in their village during the war, I became an instant celebrity! Having someone they considered very important was cause for great celebration. Kids ran around looking me over like I was a stranger from outer space.

The women gathered together and began talking excitedly. One of the men, who could speak good English, explained to me that they'd never had anyone before who was this important to visit their area, and they were trying to think of a way to honor me. To them the visit of a liberation soldier was an honor greater than the visit of the president of the country.

They had us sit down on small stools and then presented us with the best they had—a warm bottle of Coca Cola from the sari-sari store (small variety store)—as a welcome gift. As we sat, villagers came up and touched me—some with tears—to see if I was for real, and to say, "Thank you for fighting for our country."

I wished that every GI could have experienced the warmth, appreciation, and the tears of those people. For me, it was one of those rewards that made all the pain and anxiety of war worth while!

18

RECALLING GOD'S GOODNESS AT DIGDIG

As Betty and I journeyed up the highway, there were only a few lingering traces of the war. But the people remembered, and this always gave me a good feeling.

I had talked so much about Digdig, as a major objective for our regiment, that Betty could hardly wait to get there. The big disappointment was that it was just a "T" junction of two roads with a few dilapidated huts. This was one place that had not changed since the time we captured the area.

Betty and I got out of the "Glory Wagon," and hiked a short distance up a small hill. As we walked along we looked for remains of what might have been foxholes. There were indentations on the ground, so we sat down in the approximate area where I had my foxhole long ago.

"Betty, it is about here where I dug in." Then I told her about the drama in the darkness…

In 1945 there was so much talk about this place that everyone thought it was some big metropolis. When we finally got here, we discovered that there was nothing! However it was

Standing in his foxhole at Maringalo, where he earned the Silver
Star Medal on February 28, 1945. The author with his oldest
daughter Janet, and two grandchildren, January 30, 1992.

exceedingly significant in that it was a strategic point for both sides—for us and for the Japanese. This was the last convergence of major roads before going into the rugged and steep mountainous region. We were there to intercept the Japanese, who were trying to escape to the north to join Gen. Yamashita's forces.

Faithful Filipino scouts gave reports that there was a good deal of activity during dark hours, and that we should expect movement along the road every night. The report that enemy tanks were spotted put us on high alert.

As I dug in, I had a good view of the rest of the soldiers, who were digging in around the perimeter, all of which encircled the junction of the road. The "T" would be in the middle of the circle of troops.

Because of casualties, our ranks were thin. The company (originally about 200) had been depleted to less than 150 men. Being short of men and because of Filipino scout reports, we were assigned a tank destroyer unit with its vehicle—an M-7 in military language—with tank-like tracks. But it was not a tank in that it did not have a turret. Mounted on its front end was a 75 mm cannon that fired armor-piercing shells. The vehicle, with its contingent of four men, was strategically placed on the road looking south.

Any enemy tank traveling north would be in for a big surprise. But there would be a surprise tonight that would be beyond anything that we could have anticipated.

As twilight came on, we were ready. From my foxhole I could look down on the M-7, which was about thirty meters (approximately twenty-five yards) away. Every third man would be awake, as darkness settled over the area. There was little noise. Men spoke only in whispers.

As the first watch started, men began drifting off to sleep. The watch changed at 9:30 P.M. and then at 11:00 P.M. Now it was my turn to be on guard.

As always at night there was some activity. Basically the usual sound was men getting up to relieve themselves. When this happened others were quietly told: "Man in front. Hold your fire."

It was about midnight, when I heard an unnatural sound. It just was not right, but it only lasted for a second or two. It sounded like somebody had tripped over something—even like two steel pieces hitting together. There was some shuffling, and then all was quiet.

At daylight there was excited talking, which woke me up. Down by the tank destroyer there was all kinds of activity. Guys were taking turns going down to see what had happened. One of the men from my squad had just returned. He said that in the middle of the night an enemy soldier had tried to infiltrate our lines, and a member of the tank destroyer unit had killed the infiltrator.

I went down to investigate, and sure enough there was a dead Japanese soldier, lying on the edge of a foxhole. There was no question about it. He was after the tank destroyer.

The man on watch heard someone approaching his hole, but as often happens, men get disoriented in the night. He figured that one of our own men had gotten confused. But then he said to himself: *Something is wrong!*

He thought fast: *How do I know who this man is? Let's see— American soldiers wear combat boots with leather tops. The Japanese wear shoes that are like mittens; the big toe is separated from the rest of the toes, and they wear cloth-wrapped leggings.*

Then he acted. In the blackness of the night our soldier reached out and gently touched the legging of the visitor. In a flash he came up with the butt of his rifle, caught the invader under the chin, and then came down with a crash on his head. It was all over in seconds, and the enemy was dead. When daylight came, it was discovered that he was a *kamikaze* soldier with dynamite strapped to his body. He was bent on destroying the M-7, himself, and as many Americans as possible!

The chilling reality is that if this enemy soldier had succeeded in his mission, the explosion of the dynamite on his body would have ignited other high explosive shells in the tank destroyer, and this in turn would have killed everyone within fifty meters or more. It would have surely killed me, because on guard duty I would always sit on the edge of my hole. Being so close, the concussion would have blown me into eternity.

There is no question about it. God once more had spared my life because of the quick thinking and action of a fellow soldier. He was decorated with a medal for his courageous act.

Betty and I prayed together, and thanked the Lord for His protection. She said, "Just think if that Japanese had succeeded with his mission, we would never have known each other, or had the opportunity of being here."

We were grateful to the Lord for the privilege of being on Philippine soil reliving this scene together.

19

REMEMBERING MIRACLES ALONG HIGHWAY 5

It was early afternoon when we left Digdig and headed toward Santa Fe, which would be our destination for the night. It was another road junction, and a strategic objective during the war.

As we drove through the foothills, I was eagerly looking for reminders of the war to point out to Betty. In this area I was full of nostalgia. Almost every hill reminded me of some event. But I was looking for specifics—landmarks of miracles—the Bulldozer Road and Putlan Bridge, which I planned to mention in my talks at the conference.

We drove between two small hills that I immediately recognized. There on my left was Bryant Hill, named by the Philippine government in honor of a Private Bryant. His only weapon turned out to be a defunct flame-thrower.

On a hill on the right side of the road our squad was lying flat on our stomachs, waiting for our next orders.

Across the road and on the hill to the left, we could see a rather boring situation. Men were in the same position that we were in.

But quickly things caught our attention, and became exciting. Bryant, about whom we knew exactly nothing at the time, and the rest of his squad started to advance. The enemy, entrenched along the crest of the hill, opened fire and pinned them all down. Bryant was near a bunker, and gave it a blast of flame. The enemy fired back with their automatic weapons, wounding Bryant. Then to our amazement, his flame-thrower burned out. But this didn't stop him. We saw him stand up and run toward the enemy, swinging the nozzle of his weapon. Bullets cut him down again and again, but he got up and kept going. He reached the enemy lines and then disappeared.

As far as we knew, that was the end. However, we later learned that his heroics were outstanding. His single-handed effort killed eighteen of the enemy before he was mortally wounded. When his squad took the hill, it found the whole contingent of Japanese had been wiped out. Bryant was awarded the Medal of Honor posthumously.

As we moved along the twisting, turning road, the terrain became more and more treacherous. Just looking up the cliffs and ridges that rise to two and three thousand feet made my hands sweat. As I thought about the struggle to gain the top of those heights, and the extreme difficulty of fighting an enemy that was dug in and waiting for us, I was reminded again of the cost of those mountains in terms of lives lost.

And there was Mt. Myoko, which we named "Maggot Hill." (See chapter 9 about details.) We couldn't really see it because of low clouds, but I knew the general vicinity. I was tempted to try to find it, but it would have been impossible, since eight years of jungle growth would have all but obliterated the trail.

Going through the deep canyons and lofty mountains, I pointed out "Bulldozer Road." The cut could still be seen, although the jungle was beginning to take over. And then we arrived at Putlan Bridge. There was no way that I could miss that. However, the road now crossed on a new bridge. Betty had already heard about these two places several years ago, but it

One of the highlights of that drive was Bryant Hill, where after running out of fuel, a private first class from the 2nd battalion hit the last of twenty-six Japs on the head with the nozzle to his flame-thrower.

was good to stop, and reflect on God's goodness. She would hear the details again at the conference.

About an hour later we arrived at Balete Pass. The Philippine government changed the name to Dalton Pass, in honor of our commanding general, who was hit and killed by a sniper's bullet in the back of his head. I recounted the events to Betty...

Word was passed along to move off the trail and give way for the general. Ahead of us was the last high ridge and major obstacle before we could look down into the Cagayan Valley and the Santa Fe junction. The general came up to survey the situation, and to decide on a strategy to take the mountain with its massive undergrowth and outcropping of rock. Conquest of this mountain would signal that we had reached the ultimate high point for the campaign. After taking this objective, we would finally have the upper hand—fighting downhill from then on.

My place on the trail was about thirty-five meters from the front line when he walked by. The general's clean uniform set him apart, and I am sure a sniper was just waiting for someone who looked important to come along. We all heard the shot. Men spotted the sniper in a tree just behind my resting place. A hail of bullets sent him tumbling from his perch, and to his own death. We were shocked. It was hard to believe that a general could die just like a private. We had lost not only our general, but a brave and daring leader.

It was a sobering lesson. We had been told over and over again: "Every man is dispensable and bullets are no respecter of rank. Regardless of your position, you must move out without respect for your life. There will always be someone to take your place." Those words were indelibly impressed on my mind, as I saw the general slump to the ground. The reality of those words became true that early morning.

At the pass we found the monument that was erected in honor of the Twenty-fifth Division. We just had to stop and read it.

**ERECTED IN
HONOR OF THOSE
SOLDIERS OF THE
25th DIVISION WHO
SACRIFICED THEIR
LIVES IN WINNING
THIS DESPERATE
STRUGGLE.**

BALETE PASS

**IN TAKING THIS PASS 7,403
JAPS COUNTED KILLED 2,365
25Th DIV. KILLED AND WOUNDED.**

MAY 13, 1945

These numbers do not include the enemy who were sealed in over two hundred caves and bunkers, which we had blown shut by dynamite. That number will only be revealed at the resurrection.

After an overnight in Santa Fe, we arrived at Aritao, and were greeted by an enthusiastic group of Christians. It was exciting to be a part of this three-day conference, since it was taking place in the very town where our division was relieved of its combat duty, after 165 days of continuous combat.

Participants were especially pleased that a missionary would travel 280 km. (approximately 175 miles) to share with them. Early on I was asked if this was my first trip to the Philippines, and that did it! When they learned that I was a member of Gen. MacArthur's liberation forces, they were overjoyed! I was a double-honored guest! I almost felt like a saint.

The evening before my first session, one of the leaders asked me to spend some time reflecting on the war. Everyone had lots of questions. Why did they have to endure such pain? Why would God allow so many of our people to die? Do you think the war was a judgment from God on us? It was evident that although the war was over eight years ago, these people were still struggling with the war's impact. That night the Lord gave me some answers for the next day.

I told a somewhat humorous incident that took place at the beginning of the Santa Fe Trail, which was identified by some as the Old Spanish Trail. They all knew it, because it was an alternative route across the mountains to the Luzon plains and on to Manila.

I shared, "Up until we came into this valley we had not taken a prisoner. But on this specific day, when the patrol went up the Old Spanish Trail, there would be a surprise.

"We were quietly moving along through tall grass with great caution. We rounded a curve, and there he was! An emaciated and half-starved Japanese soldier with his pants around his ankles, squatting on the ground to relieve himself! He had left his rifle against a tree on the other side of the path. As soon as he saw us, he began to hop like a rabbit with his pants around his ankles, to get his rifle. But it was too late. We grabbed his weapon, and we had our first prisoner!"

The people thought it was a great story, and laughed uproariously. (Unfortunately, this account showed that I still carried anger and the spirit of revenge toward the Japanese. I had absolutely no respect or compassion for them. The Lord had to take me a long way before my heart would have pity for these people.)

Then I launched into my talk giving my personal testimony of how the Lord had brought me to the Philippines as a missionary. Then when I began to mention Balete Pass, Digdig, Mt. Myoko, Carranglan, the Bulldozer Road, and Putlan Bridge, I had their complete attention.

I asked: "How many of you have traveled the road over the pass and on to Manila? Did you ever stop to read the monument?" They nodded with understanding.

I continued, "I was notified that I had been awarded the Silver Star medal for action on February 28, 1945, and was given

The author and his driver, Jesse, on January 25, 1954 at the Balete Pass monument, erected in honor of those who died in taking the pass. (Picture taken by Betty Holsinger)

the medal in late June 1945. In July of that same year, I was chosen to be one of the soldiers sent to represent the 25th Division, and to dedicate the monument (see next page). In my heart I was excited to come back to this pass. It was a personal reason because I wanted to give thanks to the Lord in the very place where we had such a life-and-death struggle.

"I wandered away from the group to a quiet place to express my thanks to my heavenly Father for His faithfulness. For me it was like the account in the Old Testament where Abraham went on top of Mt. Moriah to sacrifice his son Isaac. God spared Isaac's life, and God did the same thing with mine—I was alive because of Him!

"These mountains and this pass are holy ground. This is where the Lord's mercy was extended to me in many ways. There was no question in my mind that my heavenly Father was watching over me.

"I am sure you have given thought to Jonah's story in the Old Testament. The important thing about that account is that God was willing to use a storm, a giant fish, and an enemy nation to reveal His faithfulness, justice, and mercy. In many ways I believe that God used the war to speak to many people, including the Filipinos and myself—and even the Japanese.

"Do you realize that if it was not for the war, I would not be here as a missionary? Maybe one purpose of World War II was to show me—an individual—His care, and bring me back here again to share the Gospel with you people.

"In what way has God shown you, in terms of your own experience, the blessings of the war?

"For one thing, the war brought thousands of soldiers to your country. Many of these men caught the vision of missions on Philippine soil. Today those men are scattered throughout the world serving the Lord. But it all started here. It might seem strange, but I think that God had allowed a war to take place so that there would be a multiplication of laborers in His harvest field."

Dedication of the monument at Balete Pass (later named Dalton Pass after our general who was killed by a sniper nearby). The author is standing next to the man with the flag.

Then I shared with them what I called the monuments to miracles along the path of battle to Balete Pass.

The Putlan Bridge was one of those monuments. It was one of the major objectives after Digdig. We were racing to get there before the Japanese could destroy it. As we rounded the last curve and came in sight of the bridge, there was a tremendous blast. The Japanese were waiting. They had laced the girders with dynamite, and blew it up. We saw it crumble into millions of pieces. In one way it was a great disappointment because it would mean slowing down the delivery of supplies, which in turn would slow up our advance. The good thing is that we were able to take the area without a man being killed or wounded.

I continued, "Why was this bridge important to me? After it was destroyed, we turned upstream and fought for two weeks to capture a ridge. Our company was down from 250 to less than 100 men (see picture on next page)!

"The brutal reality of the war had shut down my emotions. Because of the loss of so many comrades and the emotional strain, I was at the place where I could not cry any more! I begged the Lord to help me cry again. The emotional build-up was so great, I thought I would explode. I told the Lord that I would never be ashamed to show my emotions in public, if I could just cry once more. The next day in the middle of the night, I was on guard duty when the tears began to flow. I was healed!

"I realized that crying, especially for men, is a gift from God. It is a beautiful gift, and a great lesson learned from the war on the banks of the Putlan River. So Putlan Bridge is a monument in my life. There I made a promise to say: 'Thank you, Lord,' every time I cried. (This commitment has been kept to this day.)

I went on to share, "As Betty and I were driving up here, I saw the remains of the cut on the side of the hill that identified the area as Bulldozer Road." (I could see the people acknowledge the place by nodding their heads.) "In that area is where

This was taken at Putlan Bridge. All that was left of the company—
less than 100 men! The author is in the back row, second from left.

The Japs destroyed Putlan Bridge in the 35th's face, so we felt that prize had been lost.

the headquarters of our battalion (a tactical unit consisting of three infantry companies and other support units) and aid station were located. That area is very special to me. The road is like an arrow pointing up the mountain to the place where God miraculously saved me from an exploding enemy mortar shell.

"We moved up the ridge with no resistance. At the top it was decided that our company would establish a perimeter and hold the ground. Unknown to us, the enemy was only a few meters away. Immediately over the crest of the ridge was a small valley backed by another ridge. The whole territory was covered with heavy vines and jungle growth under which the enemy had a network of tunnels and fortifications.

"We dug in that afternoon with a sense of safety. My foxhole was on the opposite side from the jungle area—on the back and the downside of the ridge—I could see the battalion headquarters about five hundred meters away. My place on the perimeter was open and free from the heavy undergrowth. As the day came to a close, I sensed that I was in a relatively secure place.

"The next day started out quietly, but in the afternoon snipers began to target us. They would shoot only once in a while, but their accuracy was right on target. This forced all of our men on the jungle side to crawl on their hands and knees, and sometimes on their stomachs to the safety of their holes or the downside of the ridge where I was dug in. By the end of the day two men were wounded, and a third one was dead.

"The next morning a patrol went out into the jungle, and ran into enemy fire a short distance from the perimeter. At the same time the patrol discovered the hidden fortifications, and reported back that the enemy had solid defenses on the next ridge over.

"The Japs were dangerously close. In the night, they crawled through the jungle without making any noise—and close enough to our positions to harass us with small-arms fire and grenades. The next day two more men were picked off and killed by snipers. The order still remained. We were to hold our position at any cost. However, something had to be done.

"An interesting strategy was devised, which would be one of the great acts of bravery that we would experience during the whole war. It would come from the Filipinos, who carried supplies to the front, and the wounded and dead to the rear.

"The plan was this. The American soldiers—some from their own foxholes, but others moving out toward the jungle area—would lay down a continuous blanket of fire so as to keep the heads of the enemy down. Then the Filipinos with their long, sharp bolos would walk out into the no man's land and cut down the underbrush. The clearing would force the enemy snipers to distance themselves far enough away so that they could not easily get us into their rifle sights.

"Our bullets were flying over the heads of our faithful Filipino comrades, as they worked. We could see the flash of the sun reflected off the swinging bolo blades. What a great sight. At night these brave men slept inside our perimeter, and then moved out in the morning to continue their work. This was repeated two days in a row, until the Filipinos were cutting the jungle dangerously close to the Japanese positions!

"The strategy worked, and lives were saved. The snipers continued to shoot, but the distance was so great that it was difficult to zero in adequately on moving targets.

"In many ways the bolo was as effective as the rifle, when it came to saving lives and defeating the enemy. What was especially gratifying was that not one Filipino lost his life during those two days.

"It was about a week later that the enemy intensified their harassment. They wounded three men, and killed two. After this it was decided by battalion headquarters that on the next day we would launch our own offensive.

"Our squad would lead the attack in the morning. At full strength this would be twelve men, but due to casualties we were down to six. In the afternoon, our squad leader met with the company commander to get the battle plan, which he would share with us.

"It was getting along toward evening, when I returned to the squad from an assignment. Since I had not eaten supper, our squad leader had us all gather at my foxhole. I would prepare my meal while we talked. This evening I warmed my rations with canned heat, which was lighted with a match, and would burn with a blue flame. Since any kind of light—even in twilight hours—could give our position away to the enemy, I put the fire between my legs on the bottom of my hole.

"In the middle of our discussion it happened! The last thing I remember was leaning over to stir my meal, when there was a horrendous explosion. It was a mortar shell that none of us expected. I felt like everything inside my head had been blown out! I thought I was in heaven—the birds were singing! Then consciousness brought me back to reality.

"I staggered to my feet. The squad had been destroyed! One man, from another squad, who had been sitting in his hole next to mine was wounded. But the five in my squad were gone—two died instantly, two died before my eyes, and I noticed that the fifth man had only one leg left! It was a sickening sight—blood gushing from wounds, bodies torn beyond recognition, and a buddy trying to get to his feet with only one leg! I stood there bewildered, and went into shock.

"I couldn't remember anything. When I came to consciousness I was convulsing with tears, shaking uncontrollably, and being led by two soldiers to the evacuation jeep. Everything went blank again. Then I found myself sitting in the first-aid jeep with two stretchers on both sides of me—Bill, who had lost his leg, was laid on one; on the other was a surprise. My friend Henry, from another platoon. I learned that a sniper's bullet had hit him, and left him with a shattered right upper arm and shoulder. He moaned and gave me a whispered greeting.

"That night Bob Muzzy, the sergeant in charge of the battalion aid station, was waiting to take care of me! Several months earlier we had met on New Caledonia. His brother-in-law, who was a classmate of mine at Wheaton College, suggested he try to find me. And he did.

"At our first meeting on Luzon, I had just come off the front—haggard and exhausted. My clothes were smelly, filthy, and covered with dirt. In exchange for my dirty uniform, he gave me his clean one. (He did this on four different occasions.) This act of brotherly love touched me beyond words. Tears filled my eyes. It was amazing how much this gift of a fresh uniform lifted my spirits. As I left, he assured me: 'Chuck, when your company is under fire, I will be praying. You can also count on me to be at the aid station, if there are casualties.'

"As the three of us were being unloaded, there was Bob! Along with several others, we were laid out on stretchers at the first-aid station. We talked briefly to each other, as we waited for sleep medication. Bob and the doctor gave me a sedative and then moved on to Henry, who had called him over. He wanted to talk about his wound.

"I heard Henry pleading, 'Doc, please don't amputate my arm. Do you think you'll have to amputate?'

"The doctor kindly responded, 'We'll make the decision in the morning. But now you need to rest.'

"Under heavy sedation Henry was struggling: 'Doc, if you can't give me a positive answer now, I'll die tonight.'

"The doctor tried to assure him. Then along with Bob they moved on to the other wounded men.

"Henry and I had met for the first time in boot camp. What drew us together was our church background. We often talked about home, which had a special appeal to him, since he had a fiancée back in the States. He would often pull out her picture, and we would discuss her attributes together.

"We had also talked about what our attitude should be, if we were wounded. I remember him telling me on more than one occasion that if he ever was maimed, he would not go home.

"Henry rolled over and said, 'Chuck, I think they are going to take my arm tomorrow morning. I am going to die tonight.'

"Our conversation was interrupted by a call from Bill. He desperately wanted a cigarette. I called an aid man to bring a pack and matches. In spite of my wooziness and my trembling hands, I got the smoke going via my own mouth, and then placed it in Bill's mouth.

"Bill was special. He came from Alabama. He never had a pair of shoes on in his life until he joined the Army. He couldn't read or write! How he ever got into the army no one really knows. We became friends, and as this relationship grew, I became his 'scribe.' I would read the letters from his family, and then he would dictate letters to me, which would be sent to his mother and sisters. His dad had died when he was very young.

"Many times I had shared the Lord with him, and had encouraged him by reading to him from his own New Testament, which although he couldn't read, he carried in his pocket over his heart. Because of the way the letters from home were written, I knew that there were believers in his family, and that his mom was praying for him.

"Bill asked, 'How badly am I hurt?'

"It was difficult to give a direct answer because I knew one of his legs was gone, but I tried: 'Bill, you have a severe injury, but the doctors will take care of you in the morning.'

"He then said, 'Take a look at my wound. What do you see?'

"I pulled back the blanket from his body. The wound was covered with gauze, oozing blood. It was ghastly, and gave me a sick feeling. Not only was his leg gone, but so was part of his pelvic bone. It was amazing that his internal organs were still in place.

"I staggered back to my stretcher, and said something like this: 'Bill, it's pretty bad. But I think there will be… there will be… hope… hope in the morning…' And I was gone to dreamland!

"The sleeping pill had worn off, and there was sunshine. And there was my friend Bob standing by my stretcher. I asked him for the time. He said that it was about 10:00 A.M. I rose up on my one arm, and looked over to see how my two comrades were doing. I noted that both of them had sheets over their faces. They had died in the night!

"The only way that I could react was to cry. Bob tried to comfort me, but he was of little help. He did give me more medicine, and I slept for a long time. When I woke up again, my friend said that I had been asleep for about twenty hours. He checked me over and then evacuated me to a field hospital. I spent the next two weeks there and then returned to my company.

"In reflecting on this experience there was no question that my heavenly Father was watching over me—He had saved my life, and also I had a Christian friend standing by me when I faced my greatest trauma. I thanked the Lord for His faithfulness. But I began to wonder and question again why God had spared my life."

In my final session at the conference, I shared with them about the Battle for Capintalan Ridge and "Maggot Hill" (See chapter 9).

The people had given me their undivided attention. When I finished, they applauded. There were tears, and expressions of appreciation that I would share so intimately with them.

The Lord had bonded our hearts together. There were private conversations after the main meeting. I didn't answer all of their questions, but I sensed there was a new perspective about the war, and it wasn't all negative. The conference ended on a high note. Betty and I drove away with a new appreciation of just what these people had endured during the war.

20

ANOTHER JAPANESE INVASION?

EARLY 1954

There was exciting news in the air! But it wasn't all positive. I told myself: *This can 't be. It is an affront to the Filipino people. How in the world can this government do this to its citizens and to me!* The Japanese were being invited to come again!

This news stirred up emotions and controversy. The Philippine government was proposing that the country be opened to a contingent of Japanese visitors to discuss future trade relations! Newspaper editorials were divided on the issue, and there was heated debate on the radio. (At this time there was no TV.)

What was proposed made me angry—let the enemy in again? I stood on the side of the people. We didn't want those Japanese to visit Manila, even if it would be good for business, and improve trade.

The issue also involved the Japanese government cleaning up Manila Bay, and salvaging the fifty or more sunken ships that had been sent to the bottom during the war. At this time, Manila Bay looked like a huge graveyard, with masts of sunken ships appearing above the water like crosses in a cemetery.

For some time small numbers of Japanese had been coming and going quietly, negotiating trade agreements, and proposing reparations. But now there would be a bolder move. The plan was to have a token group come from Japan as a gesture of friendship. This contingent would serve as a symbol of peace. They were to express sorrow over the war, and their statement would signify that all hostilities were over.

The Japanese had recently agreed to pay reparations in terms of millions of dollars for damages that the Philippines sustained because of the war. This was good news, and I secretly said in my heart, *I hope they pay until it hurts!*

Now the day had come. This would be the time when the enemy would once again walk down the streets of Manila!

My wife and I were in the lobby of the Manila Hotel waiting for a friend to join us. Together we would watch the parade spectacle.

There were a number of foreigners going in and out of the lobby. Among them were some Japanese. It upset me to see these people, especially those who seemed to be happy.

In the past nine years after the war I had continued to struggle with anger and resentment toward this people. Suspicion of them always lurked in the recesses of my mind and heart. It was uncomfortable for me to be around anybody and anything that was Japanese. Even riding in an automobile with a label "made in Japan" was difficult. I did not and would not trust what they manufactured! I thought it was evil that the Filipino would think of doing business with the Japanese.

It was my hope to be rid of that anger and hate. But now in the Philippines in this kind of setting, and at this point in time, memories had come back in full force. It was impossible to shake my feelings of resentment.

Intramuros—the old walled city of Manila—was just a few blocks away from the hotel. We stepped out of the hotel and walked across Luneta Park. Both the Intramuros and the Luneta were places that triggered reminders of cruelty and mock trials by the enemy.

The thought of World War II prisoners filled my mind. It was within this area that Filipino and American soldiers were accused, tortured, and incarcerated.

The "hell hole" as we called it became very vivid. This is where over two hundred captured U.S. and Philippine soldiers were jammed into a small room, which had a grated outlet into the Pasig River. The opening would allow the room to fill almost to the top with water every time the tide came in. There was no way to avoid death by drowning. This was one of the ways the Japanese "took care of" their prisoners.

Then I remembered Bataan where the Americans surrendered to the Japanese on April 9, 1942. I had visited there just a few weeks before, and walked the area so that I could get a feel of what my fellow soldiers endured. I could feel the anguish of defeat and the sneers of the conquerors. This was where the infamous Bataan Death March started, where eighteen thousand soldiers[1] were prodded, beaten, and forced to march without food or water for some 105 km. (65 miles). Brave Filipinos watching along the road risked their lives to give water to the hungering and suffering troops. Those Filipinos who were caught were pierced with a Japanese bayonet. Along the route Japanese stripped the Americans of everything they had on, even rings on their fingers, and forced them to walk naked in the blazing sun. If a soldier couldn't remove his ring, the Japanese had a simple solution—just cut the finger off! If a soldier couldn't keep going, the enemy reacted with a bayonet through his heart.

At this time of year the sun is unrelenting in its heat, and without mercy. April and May are viciously hot months. Thousands of men who succumbed to the heat were beaten to death and bayoneted along the route. Over half of the men died before they reached the prison camp.

I learned about all this firsthand from a fellow missionary, Jesse Miller, a soldier who endured the death march, and who after the war returned to the Philippines as a missionary.

It took a great deal of self-control on my part to be civil toward this enemy. What they did to the American captives and the conquered people of the Philippines was sheer horror. Having myself seen the brutality of the Japanese army, it is easy to understand the feelings of both Americans and Filipinos.

My biggest problem was trying to forget. I could not. I reminded myself again, as I had done dozens of times before: *It was the Japanese who started the war. We—Americans and Filipinos—merely finished it.* I felt that what needed to be done was to make the enemy pay dearly for their misdeeds. If I had my way, the enemy should either be snubbed, or have verbal abuse heaped on them. We should drive one more nail into the "coffin" of their defeat.

I told myself: *It is my right to be angry. Think of all the good years you missed, Chuck, because of the war.* I even thought that this attitude had some Christian virtue in it!

My mind was racing. Every time I saw a Japanese I would think, *Does this Jap know what his or her people did to the Americans and Filipinos?* Nothing but torture awaited any soldier who fell into the hands of the army that he or she represents.

And what about the Filipinos? I know how they felt and still do, regarding the accounts of abuse against their comrades-in-arms and the Filipino people!

I reflected often on how, if I had a chance to interact, I would blast these people. I would rip them with words. I would do all I could to destroy them. When I had finished with them, they would be buried under a pile of accounts of atrocities and evil.

As we stood on the parade route, I was as taut as a guitar string. One by one the events of 1945 came together again. As I dredged up memories from the recesses of the past, each picture was graphically outlined. Everything was so real that I could almost smell the war zone! I could visualize bleeding and torn bodies, and the gaunt faces of men and women stressed by days of threats and sleepless nights. It was the war all over again. My emotions were going out of control like a runaway train...

The sound of the marching band signaled that the "peace" contingent of Japanese was on the way. But what a shock—it was a Boy Scout troop! There were a dozen little boys approximately twelve to fourteen years old, waving Philippine flags!

I was right along with the crowd, shouting at the boys and resenting every one of them. Marching along and surrounding the boys were Philippine army soldiers with fixed bayonets at the ready position. An army tank rumbled along behind the troop for added protection. Civilians walking ahead of and on both sides of the scouts were pleading with the angry crowd to be kind, not to spit, or throw things.

I, along with the Filipinos, didn't pay any attention to the exhortation. (My wife and friend stood by silently.) We shouted, some cursed, and others hissed, spit, and threw things. There was no applause, no cheering, and no appreciation.

As the little scouts passed by me, I saw terror in their faces, and something happened inside my heart. My feelings turned from anger to sorrow, and from resentment to compassion. For the first time I began to look on the Japanese as humans. But it would still take sometime before I would acknowledge them as real people.

21

DIVINE DETOUR

Upon arriving back in the Philippines in 1953 the first thing I prayed was: "Lord, give me a difficult task. You know that I lived in the mud, struggled against the enemy, and endured physical hardships. I'm ready!"

Little did I anticipate what was in store for me when I awoke one morning in the second week of May 1954 with pains in both shoulders and sides. My complexion was turning yellow, and my strength was rapidly fading. A visit to the doctor confirmed our suspicion that I was seriously ill with hepatitis. It would mean complete bed rest and weekly visits to the doctor. The doctor consoled me by saying that the duration of such an illness would only be about two months.

When word got around the Christian community that I had hepatitis, the amoebic type, affecting my liver, it stirred up many Filipinos and fellow missionaries to visit me and pray. Several would say, "I had that once, but it only lasted four months." Another friend told me that he had hepatitis for six months, but that was a record, and surely I would be up before then.

The days and weeks went by. Rather than getting better, my condition worsened. We were into the hot season, and the heat was not helping my condition. I even anticipated dying.

After four months had passed, a surprise phone call came from Taiwan from the president of our mission. He had consulted with a missionary doctor, and their decision was to move me and my family to Taiwan. The cooler climate would enable me to have a faster recovery. (I would learn later that there was another reason.) God was taking me on a "divine detour"!

On December 28, 1954, we left the Philippines for a short stay on Taiwan. (At that time we did not know that there would be no long-term ministry for us in the Philippines for the next twenty-five years!)

TAIWAN 1955

Taipei, Taiwan was a great blessing. Almost immediately I began to sense my strength coming back under the care of Dr. Donald Dale, the OC's official doctor. He even encouraged me to take a walk every day to build up my legs. In the cool climate I began to make great strides. I was fast gaining strength, and it looked like I could become active again.

At this same time the president of our mission, Dr. Dick Hillis, paid me a surprise visit. He said, "Chuck, I have just received an invitation from the U.S. Servicemen in Okinawa to go there for a weekend conference. They want me to bring along someone to share from his life and experience. I immediately thought of you. These Air Force guys need to hear your testimony about the war. Also, Dr. Dale thinks it would be good for you."

Betty and I talked it over, and our answer was an enthusiastic "Yes!" But a few days later I began to have second thoughts. I had made up my mind never to have anything to do with the Japanese, and going to Okinawa was "invading" enemy territory! But I thought I would be "safe" from any of the enemy, since I would be with Americans only. This gave me some peace about the decision. Before long Betty and I plus our only child, Chuckie David, were on our way to Naha, Okinawa to minister to GIs.

OKINAWA, MARCH 1955

We arrived two days before the conference, and were greeted at the airport by Bob Boardman, a missionary with the Navigators, a mission agency. He and his wife would be our hosts until the conference began. We would then move to base housing. Bob's home was in a Japanese district. This made me somewhat edgy, but I went along without a complaint.

As a Marine, Bob had been a part of the battle for Okinawa. He and I bonded right away, as we shared our war experiences of being on the front line and enduring the terrors of combat. We spoke each other's language, both of the mind and of the heart. We understood each other without even trying to explain.

In the afternoon Bob whispered that he would like to take me out for a walk. He had to whisper because he had been shot through the throat by a Japanese bullet. He would never have a normal voice again. But he had come back to Okinawa to whisper the Gospel to the Japanese!

As we started on our walk, my first question to him was: "Bob, how can you come back and share the Gospel with these people, after being maimed for life by them?"

His answer startled me: "A wound like this is no worse than my sins. God forgave me my sins, so why should I not forgive the Japanese."

It was a powerful statement that left me in silence.

We followed a path that went through a meadow, across a small hill, and down into a little valley. Suddenly Bob said, "Stop!" Then surrounded by the quietness of the morning, he said in his whispered voice, "Here is where I was wounded."

He continued, "We were following this very road. See that ridge across the valley? We didn't know it, but the enemy was dug in and waiting for us. There was a blast of machine-gun fire, which cut down one of my buddies and left him lying in an exposed area. It was a dangerous situation, but we had to try and rescue him. I was able to pick him up and put his arm around my shoulder. As we tried to escape, the enemy got us in his sights from the shoulders up. The bullets ripped off my index finger and struck me in the throat. We were both rescued, but we were scarred forever."

Then he whispered, "I don't bring many people here, but I knew that you would understand. Let's sit down and pray for each other." After our prayer we sat in silence for a long time.

Then he said, "Chuck, these scars are beauty marks. They are like the nail prints in Jesus' hands. These wounds are my credentials to the Japanese people that I have forgiven them."

As we walked home our words were few. I was struggling with my own thoughts, and the tremendous example of this man. In the next few days, I could not get Bob or his words out of my mind. God would use him in a special way to help me along the road to forgiveness.

The afternoon before the conference was to begin, a chaplain asked me to join others in a prayer meeting. I was ready and eager to go. But we had a problem with transportation, so the chaplain and I arrived late.

We walked into the room, and I was stunned and furious! Some of those who were praying and kneeling in the circle were Japanese. I wanted to get out of there as quickly as possible, but there was no retreat. I took a chair near the door. I knelt like the rest of them, but I refused to pray! There was a stream of ants crawling across the floor, and I occupied myself by playing with them with my finger rather than pray.

A considerable amount of time went by, when I heard a man immediately across the room praying. His words were not in English. He was speaking in the Japanese language to my heavenly Father!

I thought of Bob Boardman. Suddenly in the quiet of my heart I heard God speak, *Chuck, that Japanese is your brother. You better forgive him, if you want to get well!*

There on my knees I asked the Lord to forgive me, and I in turn forgave the Japanese people. For the past ten years, I had carried bitterness, and anger, and even a fear of this people. But now I felt that some of this was being washed away.

A second thing happened at that meeting. The Lord gave me the assurance that I would get well. I got up from my knees feeling better. Forgiveness was beginning to heal my body, but complete emotional healing would not come until later. However, this experience was a major factor, if I was to get back to the Philippines again.

My time with the GIs was terrific. I shared: "You thought the main reason for me coming here was to speak to you. But God had a bigger purpose. He spoke to me as I listened to the prayer of a Japanese, and the testimony of a Marine!" Then I went into details concerning my experiences of the last two days.

That night I thought about God's gentleness, kindness, and gentle prodding in my life. He had brought me back to the Philippines, allowed me to get sick, moved me to Taiwan, got me an invitation to speak in Okinawa, and taught me two powerful lessons.

But there was still something wrong. I had faced up to dealing with the Japanese as a people, though not as an enemy! It would be a few more years before I would come face to face with Scripture and Jesus' words: "You have heard that it was said, 'Love your neighbor and hate your enemy.' But I tell you: Love your enemies and pray for those who persecute you, that you may be sons of your Father in heaven" (Matthew 5:43-45).

My sickness continued, and I had to return to the U.S. for two years of treatment. But instead of complaining about it to the Lord, I was thankful.

22

UNFORGETTABLE MIKE

SPRING 1969

I will never forget Mike. His attitude was amazing. He is one man who had every right to hate the Japanese for the rest of his life.

We met while aboard the same flight on China Airlines from Hong Kong to Tokyo. The plane was only partially full. Mike occupied a window seat. The seat next to him was vacant, and I was seated directly across the aisle.

I noticed that Mike had a strange way of talking. His words were always garbled and slurred, and he held his jaw all the time. It was embarrassing to hear him try to explain to the Chinese cabin attendant what he wanted for lunch.

At mealtime it was agitating to hear him eat, to say the least. The sounds of slurping were irritating. The napkin draped over his chest was covered with saliva and particles of food. This man had an etiquette problem that was beyond description!

After lunch, I glanced at him. He had taken his hand away from his chin, and I saw his problem: his chin hung down from his mouth by a piece of skin that was like a hinge.

I believe God prompted my next action. I moved across the aisle and introduced myself. His response was warm and assuring, but because of the damage to his face, it was impossible to tell whether he was smiling or scowling. We shared trivial things with each other. And then he asked me, "Is this your first time in the Orient?"

I responded, "No, I have been here many times. But my first time was as an infantry soldier with the Twenty-fifth Division. I was in Guadalcanal, took part in the invasion of Vella Lavella Island, just off the southern tip of Bougainville. Next, I was in the battle for Luzon, in the Philippines, and finally went to Japan with the occupation forces." My words had gotten through to him.

I asked, "What about you? Is this your first trip?"

"No," and then with hesitation, he said, "I was here in the war also. This is my second trip out."

I said, "Where is your destination now?"

He looked me in my eyes and his response startled me as he said: "Tokyo. I was a prisoner of war in Japan. I'm going back to tell them that I forgive them. As a former soldier I am sure you'll understand." He hesitated. "See my chin? In order to get control of the American soldiers in the prison camp, the guards picked prisoners at random to make examples out of them. I was one of those men. They said I talked too much. They took me into the infirmary, knocked me out with drugs, and cut out my jaw bone."

Now I was in shock. I looked at him but couldn't answer. Words were useless to express my emotions. I gazed at him in amazement, and through my tears I blurted out, "To tell the Japanese that you forgive them!"

He went on: "That was many years ago. I struggled with anger and resentment, because this would mean that I would never be married. My girlfriend would not accept me upon my return from the war. There was no way that I could kiss her good morning or good night meaningfully…"

I interrupted by saying, "I'm so sorry!"

He continued with more startling words: "I've been saving up my money for these past many years so I could make this trip, and give my captors my message!"

He returned from the war in 1945. Now, in 1969, he knew it was his time to act. The amazing thing is that he was free from anger, resentment, and all bitterness.

I said to myself, *This man is remarkable.* It was puzzling to me that he would go back to the people who had ruined his life.

He answered my question without my asking: "I have traced my captors and guards. I have written them that I wanted to return, and meet with them, and they have agreed."

I said, "What in the world are you going to tell them?"

His answer was simple and to the point: "I told you already. I have one message: I forgive you!"

I said, "You sound like a Christian. Are you one?"

And he answered, "No."

My response to him was out of utter amazement, "You sound like Jesus, when He was being crucified. Do you know Him? He said while He was being crucified, 'Father forgive them for they know not what they do!'"

He said, "Yes, I have heard that before."

An announcement from the cockpit came too quickly: "Return to your seats, and fasten your seat belts." And in minutes we were on the ground.

As we taxied to the tarmac, I thanked my newfound friend for his example of courage and forgiveness. My last words to him were: "You are a big man to do what you are doing. You are acting like Jesus. Someday I hope you will know Him." He nodded and smiled, as best he could.

Outside was a crowd of smartly dressed older Japanese men. I knew whom they were waiting for. I said to the ones nearest the door, "He's coming!"

They bowed and smiled, and I passed on.

I stopped and waited from a distance to see what would happen when Mike came through the door. There was a welcoming roar from the crowd. I stopped and prayed for Mike, and then moved on. One thing for sure—he, a non-Christian, had indelibly impressed on me the meaning of real forgiveness!

23

I MEET YUKIKO

EARLY 1970

The war was over twenty-five years ago. I had passed through Tokyo on a number of occasions, but it was always with feelings of uneasiness. I purposely tried to avoid any personal contact with the Japanese. After all, this was "enemy territory."

To me Tokyo was my Samaria! In St. John, chapter 4, it states that Jesus must pass through Samaria. The disciples didn't want to go there—the Samaritans were a despised enemy. But Jesus forced the issue—we must go there! I was very much like those disciples!

On trips to the Orient it was not uncommon to be seated next to a Japanese. But there was never any extended conversation. After an initial greeting of *"Konichiwa"*[1] (How are you?) or *"Ohio gazimis"* (Good morning or Good day), a smile, and a nod of the head, the conversation would end. Why talk with any of them? Even though I had forgiven them as a people, they were still an object of my suspicion.

This flight to Japan didn't quite start right. I had to run to catch my plane in San Francisco. Then on arriving in Tokyo, it was announced that the next leg of my journey had been postponed because of a storm. The airlines graciously put us all up for the night in a local hotel.

The next day when I checked in at the Narita Airport, I thought it would just be an ordinary day. I never dreamed that this would be very similar to the Samaritan encounter that the disciples experienced with Jesus. I was jolted when I found I would be seated next to an enemy.

My normal practice was to take an aisle seat, but today I would request one by the window. I had spent a restless night in the hotel, and my head was hot, and my joints hurting. It was obvious that I was coming down with a fever, and I needed sleep. A seat away from the aisle would be my best bet. I could lay my head against the window, and my sleep would be sweet until we landed in Hong Kong.

I was about to close my eyes when I discovered that my seat companion was a young Japanese woman. She gave me a warm smile as we introduced ourselves. Her name was Yukiko and she worked for the Yamaha Piano Company, teaching young people how to use the electronic keyboard. She was on her way to several schools in Hong Kong for such an assignment.

I was in no mood to talk, especially since her English was very poor. But a closer look at her startled me. I laid my head back, closed my eyes, trying to remember where and under what circumstances our paths had crossed. I said to myself, *I've seen this woman some place before.* With that strange inner feeling, I was suddenly awake.

I could sense that she wanted to practice her English on me, but I wasn't about to let that happen. There would be no sleep if I got involved. But she was a bright, alert woman, so grudgingly I decided to help her with pronunciation for a minute or two until we were airborne.

The pilot's announcement reminded me that we had been on the ground for a long time. There was a typhoon between

Japan and Hong Kong, but the captain's words were encouraging: "We will be diverting our course somewhat to the west. This will take us over the Taiwan Straits toward the Philippines, and hopefully we will skirt the storm. We are cleared for take-off, so fasten your seat belts."

Our chat continued. Her responses were always animated and cheerful: "*Hi!*" she would say with a rising inflection. This meant, "Yes, I understand."

The conversation began to drag, and I was becoming more weary. There were more and more lapses between questions, answers, and sentences. It was more difficult to stay awake.

Her next question was a simple one. In her lilting way she asked, "When you first meet Japanese?"

I looked into her bright and cheerful eyes and said, "Yukiko, I first met Japanese in World War II. I fought against your people in the South Pacific and the Philippines."

My answer was like a physical blow to her body. When she heard my statement, her face turned ashen. She grasped both armrests, and her knuckles began to turn white. Her features turned an ugly gray as the brightness left her face. I had seen that many times in the battlefield, when a fellow soldier was wounded. She was in shock!

I knew I had to say or do something. But what? Fortunately I was rescued by the pilot, who came on the inter-com and announced that we would be passing over Northern Luzon, Philippines. Below I could see the western coast of the island. The sand was a ribbon of gold. By the shape I recognized Lingayen Gulf, where I had made the landing as a soldier with thousands of other GIs. I was suddenly wide awake.

Things raced through my mind. The Japanese messed up the lives of so many Americans and Filipinos—killings, tortures, cruelty, and rape. The pain and anguish of combat, and the cry of the wounded and the dying came alive. I felt as though I was in battle again!

I pressed my face against the window, and I could see the plain of Luzon, the Caraballo mountains and two little knolls on which had been a Japanese observation post. Beyond were the towns of San Manuel and Lupao. Yes, Lupao! That was where we fought our first big battle, and I began to live it all over again. It was all so real that I could almost smell the powder of spent ammunition rounds.

Then I asked myself: *What is going on with this woman? She is too young to even have experienced the war! Who is she anyway that she should react so violently? Where, oh where, have I seen this woman before?*

But now I was sensing anger rising within me, and I began to regret that I ever chose that window seat.

I shook the cobwebs from my mind, and reality began to return as Luzon and the Philippines faded in the distance. There was about an hour left of the journey, and then I would be free from this woman forever!

As I tried to relax, something clicked in the recesses of my mind. And suddenly I remembered!—which brought goose pimples on my arms. There on the screen of my mind was the scene where I had taken a picture—a souvenir—from the pocket of the dead Japanese officer whom we had found, and killed under a bridge near Digdig! Was that a picture of this woman?

At the same time I knew I had to do something for Yukiko. I silently prayed, *Oh, Lord, help!* And the Lord brought Mike to mind! (See previous chapter.)

Looking back over the three and a half war years, which I had just lived through in less than an hour, I was reminded that I was alive today because "Somebody" had been watching over me. Yes, the battles were over, and I had survived—the tanks had missed; when pinned down by machine-gun fire, those bullets had missed; when caught in the crossfire and fusillade of tank guns—I hadn't even a scratch! I was a living evidence of God's faithfulness.

I opened my mind and in the next few moments, I saw my war deliverance, in living color. I should have been dead many times over. I thought: *What about Maggot Hill, the battle for Maringalo when the enemy had closed in within three meters of my position; and yes, the assault on Balete Pass when the intensity of the fire and grenades made it almost certain that that would be my final day on earth?*

I looked at my watch. Hong Kong was still about an hour away. The woman next to me still sat in a rigid position. It seemed like an eternity since we had last spoken to each other.

Suddenly I realized that God was answering my prayer for help. The first thought that crossed my mind was: *Chuck, maybe one great reason for the war, and you remembering Mike, is for this poor woman.*

In a still small voice God was trying to say something, and the answer was very clear; His answer was like a shout. God was trying to make me hear above my emotions. It was very simple. I could hear the Lord say, *Touch her!*

I reached out and patted her arm, and quietly said, "Yukiko, I want you to know that I forgave your people long ago."

With that word her eyes opened, and her hands began to relax. I could see sunshine return to her face, as she said, "You forgive?"

And I answered, "Yes."

Then she asked, "When you forgive?"

I told her of my journey back to the Philippines, then to Taiwan and finally to Okinawa, where my forgiveness began in a prayer meeting.

I said, "Yukiko, I believe that God has spared my life, if for no other reason than that you and I could sit together on this flight."

She responded with a smile in her voice, "*Hi!*"

I discovered that although she faltered with spoken English her understanding of the printed page was excellent. So I pulled out my Bible and showed her some verses, especially Mark 11:25: "...if you hold anything against anyone, forgive him, so that your Father in heaven may forgive you your sins."

I apologized for not speaking sooner. There was no way that I could make her understand my initial emotions, especially when the picture from the officer's pocket flashed across my mind. But she could understand forgiveness.

She accepted my forgiveness, and I accepted hers. From there we moved on to talk about what it means to be a Christian. My words were inadequate, and I could see puzzlement in her face. So I stopped trying to explain.

Instead I took her through verses in the Bible that stressed believing—John 3:16; 5:24; Acts 4:12; Romans 10:9. As we looked at the verses, I could see that she understood. There was a long pause, and then she said, "A Christian believe?"

Excitedly I said, "Yes, yes!"

She said, "*Hi!* OK, OK."

I responded, "Do you believe, Yukiko?"

And she gave a confident "Yes." Then she said, "I Christian now!" This was followed by a big smile.

We were about to land so I said, "Yukiko, can we pray together? We can talk to God!"

The prayer was simple, but I sensed that she had grasped all that we had talked about. In the airport we grasped each others' hands, and with warm smiles we parted, never to see each other again.

That encounter took the anger and bitterness for the Japanese out of my heart forever. I was so grateful that Yukiko never heard my inward battle. It would have destroyed her, but in the end she was saved. I thanked the Lord for the experience, and was certain that God understood. At last I was free! The enemy was finally forgiven. Great peace filled my innermost being.

When I returned to the States, I found the picture, looked at it one more time, and then threw it away. In God's own time and way, the picture had served its purpose.

24

HONOR BEYOND EXPECTATION

SUMMER 1974

It was suppertime in one of those noisy, crowded restaurants in Manila. I sat at a table with six other American missionaries, whom I had met for the first time that evening. The meal was over and talk was flowing freely, when one of the ladies asked me, "When did you first come to the Philippines?"

My response startled some of them: "I landed with the U.S. Army invasion force, as a liberation soldier in 1945." This started a whole series of questions about the war—battles, the Filipinos, the Japanese, and the American troops.

They wanted to know about my experiences, especially after they learned that I had been a scout (point man) on the front lines. I shared with them that I was a part of the Twenty-fifth Division, which landed at Lingayen Gulf on January 11, 1945, and then spent 165 days in continuous combat—a record for all divisions in both the Asian and European theaters of operation during World War II.

Because of the noise and chatter in the restaurant, it was necessary to raise my voice, as I spoke in detail how my life had been spared on more than one occasion, and that I was alive today because of God's faithfulness.

There was a pause, and as usual someone asked the question: "Did you ever have to shoot anybody?" I didn't answer that question forthrightly, but I did tell them that on more than one occasion, I was in no man's land. I tried to leave something for their imagination.

Then I said, "Let me tell you about a life-changing lesson that I learned from a naked little Filipino boy."

First I told them how we had landed on the beach at Lingayen Gulf, and pushed inland about two miles to establish a perimeter of defense that would be the dividing line between our armed forces and the enemy (See chapter 2).

But the Japanese came up with a new tactic that really shook us all up—*the kamikaze*—suicide soldiers! I then told them the account of a *kamikaze* rounding up a group of eight Filipino men, and under the guise of wanting to surrender, asked them to escort him to the American lines (See chapter 3). Then having gained entrance into the perimeter he pulled the detonator pin causing the death of many. With this background I launched into my story—

"Three days later, I was on perimeter guard when a group of Filipinos emerged from a bamboo thicket about fifty meters away, and called out to be waved in. Immediately we were all on the alert. With rifles ready, each soldier including myself called out which man he had targeted to shoot. The sergeant yelled, 'I have the first one.' The next soldier shouted, 'I have the second one.' This was done as a new person stepped out from the bamboo.

"After the main group had cleared the thicket, there was additional movement in the bamboo. We clicked off our safeties, and were ready to spray the bamboo with rifle fire. In that moment the leader of the group screamed out: 'Don't shoot, it's my brother!'

"It was showdown time! We cautiously waved the group toward our lines, and then called for the brother, or whomever he might be in the thicket, to advance and be recognized. There was skepticism about who this was who was still in the bamboo thicket.

"Out stepped a naked boy about twelve years old! The brother explained that he was too embarrassed to come forward with the others, because he wore no clothes.

"We called the little boy to join us and then the joy began! One soldier ran and got him a T-shirt. Another handed him a candy bar. He couldn't speak English, but through his brother he tried to say, 'Thank you.'

"In the midst of the celebration the little boy whispered something to his brother. The brother in turn announced to the assembled soldiers, which now numbered twelve or fourteen, that his little brother wanted to thank us all by singing a song.

"The boy now dressed in his 'new clothes,' which looked more like a dress than a shirt, started singing at the top of his voice in Tagalog. Because he was straining so hard, the jugular vein in his neck and the blood vessels in his head looked like they would burst! We didn't understand a word, but now and then we thought we caught a garbled thank-you.

"After six or seven verses, the little boy's voice began to give out, and we pleaded with the brother to stop him. It was no use. The boy went on until his voice was only a whisper. He was exhausted, but there was no question about it—he was thankful! The older brother explained, 'My brother wanted to make sure that he had said thank-you enough!'

"This was an experience of legendary dimension—a little naked boy got through to us soldiers, and to me especially. I have made this experience a cornerstone in my life. So many times there are good things—surprises—that are provided by our heavenly Father—new friends, a reaffirmation of His faithfulness, a sunset—which we take for granted. But we can never thank the Lord too much!"

It was now time to leave the restaurant. I pushed back my chair and as I stood up, a young Filipina, probably in her late thirties and a total stranger, approached me. She had been sitting at the table next to ours. I could see tears in her eyes.

She said, "Sir, please excuse me. I have been listening to your stories. I want to express my thanks to you for fighting for my country and liberating us!" Then she choked up.

I said, "But you are too young to have experienced the war."

She replied with little tears trickling down her cheeks, "Yes, I know, but I have never had the opportunity to express my appreciation in person to a soldier who actually fought for my country."

She paused, and then haltingly she continued, "Sir, may I shake your hand?"

I held out my hand. She grabbed it with both of hers, and all she could say through her tears was, "Thank you, thank you, thank you."

After she gained her composure, she said, "I overheard that you are a Christian. I also am one. This makes me even more appreciative, especially that you are here now to share your life with my people."

In a small way at that moment I sensed a bit of how Jesus must have felt when Mary Magdalene anointed His feet with expensive perfume. This dear lady had done a similar act to me.

I went away moved in the depths of my heart.

Dad and Mother with grandchildren visit Philippines, 1958.

25

APPRECIATION BEYOND WORDS

JUNE 1980

One of the greatest tributes I have received in my lifetime came about forty years after Gen. MacArthur had fulfilled his vow, "I shall return," to the Philippines and had brought several of us with him into the country!

This was during one of the more than forty trips I would make to this country after World War II. On these occasions, every older Filipino who knew of my history always expressed appreciation. But this trip would be different.

I was in the company of other Americans high in the mountains at the Baguio City airport. The plane was late, and we were all restless and bored. We had arrived at 5:00 A.M. for the 6:00 morning departure, but the flight was late. To kill time we all decided to enlist the services of a little shoeshine boy, who was twelve years old. The seven of us would get a shine.

I was the last in line. We didn't know the nature of the conversation between the interpreter and the little boy, but we learned later that he was briefing the boy regarding whose shoes he was shining. As he worked his way down the line, I watched his little efficient fingers rub in the wax and then buff each shoe. He had the same ritual for each person. Beads of sweat stood out on his forehead as he tried to make each shoe like new.

When he came to me, things changed. He gave me a big smile, and then through the interpreter, asked me to remove my shoes. From his pocket he pulled out a soiled cloth that he had used to wipe the perspiration from his face, placed it on the floor, smoothing it out, oh so carefully. Then to my surprise, he asked that I stand on his makeshift handkerchief. I hesitated, but he persisted. He shined my shoes and as he did, he kept looking up at me with a smile, and would periodically say, "Thank you, sir." It was the only English he knew.

When the job was over, he refused to take my money. I asked the interpreter what was going on. I learned that he had told the boy I was a soldier of Gen. MacArthur's liberation forces, and had fought in the mountains west of Baguio.

The interpreter explained that this little boy, whose only knowledge of the war was hearsay because of his age, wanted to say, "Thank you for fighting for my country." My free shine and the special way he did it was his way of letting me know that he appreciated the American soldiers.

After the shine was finished, he stood by me in silence until our plane arrived. We boarded and as we taxied away, I could see his hand clutching the little cloth and waving it, as his lips kept saying, "Thank you."

26

UNEXPECTED SURPRISE

SPRING 1988

I t was May—summertime in Manila—and extra hot. There was a short rain, and as usual the streets were steaming with heat. To add to our discomfort, it was about 10:00 A.M., one of the hottest hours of the day. We were in the slums of Tatalon District in Quezon City in Metro Manila, and the thought of World War II was the furthest thing from my mind.

We were being given a tour of a special project for the poor. Streets were in desperate need of repair. Trash littered the area, and there was the slight but distinct smell of sewage. The places the people called "home" were shanties made from scraps of wood, and their roofs from rusty corrugated iron weighted down with old rubber tires.

We were met by a young pastor with two small children tugging at his hands. He and his wife served the community at great sacrifice living among the people.

Conditions were deplorable—hordes of flies, clogged sewers, and pungent odors. But this pastor had committed himself and his family to meet the needs of these people. His ministry included a preschool and an on-the-job training program.

After our tour, we were invited to his home to have a drink. His wife immediately disappeared out the front door and quickly returned with a bottle of warm Coca Cola, a favorite but costly drink, especially for those who live at such an extremely low poverty level. But this was Filipino hospitality—nothing but the best for the guests!

In the course of the conversation the subject came up as to when I had first come to the Philippines. I said, "It was forty-three years ago."

I could almost see her mind working, as she sorted out the numbers and then the dates. She quickly said, "But that was liberation time! I wasn't even born yet!"

I said, "Yes, you are right. I first came to your country as a liberation soldier."

She then did something that startled us all. She got up from her chair, came across the room, knelt down before me, and grasped my hand. With tears trickling down her cheeks, she said, "Thank you. Thank you for fighting for our country so that we could be free." She hung on to my hand with head bowed for a second or two, as though she was praying. I responded with a warm smile and a pat on her hand, then she stood up and returned to her chair.

The conversation moved to other things, and then it was time to go. As we prepared to depart, the wife said, "Would you accept a small gift of appreciation for being a liberation soldier?"

Not knowing what to expect, I said, "Yes, I would be more than happy to receive something from you." She disappeared into the kitchen, and returned with a banana.

As she presented the banana to me she said, "We don't have very much, but I want you to know how grateful I am for your sacrifice. I know the war must have been difficult for you."

What a tribute! I was emotionally touched, and left speechless. But in that moment I was reminded of the Bible story where the widow dropped two pennies into the offering box. And in the Lord's sight it was more than what the rich ones gave. This Christian sister had given a Coke and a banana, which she and her husband could hardly afford! I am sure her deed is recorded in heaven.

Little sister, Laura, in Ifugao Country, 1956.

27

STUNNING TURNABOUT

MAY 1990

In May of 1999 the war would descend on my mind and heart with full force. But on this weekend it would be a different kind of feeling. There would be no anger, no hate, no feeling of revenge towards the Japanese. This had been buried long ago. Now I longed that my Filipino brothers and sisters, who continued to carry bitterness toward the Japanese—their enemy—would learn to forgive.

Since 1980 our organization, Philippine Crusades (changed to Philippine Challenge in 1992), had been conducting pastors' conferences, focusing on instructions on church planting. The speakers were missionaries like myself, plus national workers, who had been successful at planting new churches. My assignment in these gatherings was to provide inspiration and encouragement from the Bible. I was to speak three times during the conference.

The venue was the Central Luzon State University (CLSU) campus, which flanked the highway (the old Highway 5) leading north through Nueva Ecija province, passing through the cities of Cabanatuan and San Jose, over the Caraballo mountains and into the Cagayan Valley.

I arrived for the three-day conference early on a Thursday afternoon. The conference would start the next day so this would give me plenty of time to rest and be prepared.

I decided to go out for a walk along the road, and suddenly my thoughts went back to the war. I had walked that road as an infantry soldier! I could remember the apprehension and anxiety of walking into uncertainty, the stress, the fatigue, even the taste of spent gunpowder. My heart started pounding, and the palms of my hands broke out into a sweat. My emotions surprised me. I quickly retreated from the road and busied myself with other things.

That evening my mind was so full of the war that I could not sleep. I tossed and turned all night. I was up at daybreak, went out by the road, and sat under a tree to await the rising sun. I had taken my Bible along, and started to look up the verses that had meant so much to me during the war. As I did this, the Lord gave me a thought of what I should share with the pastors. My message would be on forgiveness, and I would reinforce it with stories from my war experiences.

In a conference like this, my opening remarks were always the same: "Good morning, pastors, I am honored to be here. The first time I set foot on this island was as an infantry soldier in 1945. I came back with Gen. MacArthur's liberation forces."

With this kind of an introduction there would be an instant quietness of almost sacred silence. The attendees would stop talking. A hush would come over the crowd, and I would have every person's attention. Then I would share several stories and move on to my message.

However, because of the special setting of this conference I felt led to talk only about forgiveness. The background and illustrations would be very vivid.

Most of these pastors would remember the war, even though they would have been very young. At the same time the anguish and devastation of the war would really grip their minds and hearts, as they heard about the war once again. I also knew that many of them had never forgiven the Japanese, the enemy, and the war had happened over forty years ago!

I felt the same way that Jesus and His disciples felt when He said to the Pharisees, "If they keep quiet, the stones will cry out" (Luke 19:40). I had to cry out…

"Brothers and sisters, your country is very sacred to me. I have been back here many times. In fact this is my forty-sixth visit. And I have personally come to this area a number of times since the war. In 1958 I walked the battle areas with my parents, wife, and children. We stood together in the very foxholes that I had dug, and lifted our hearts in gratitude for God's faithfulness. I can still find some of those foxholes to this day! The battle and events have impacted me forever. These are sacred places—almost like the Bible lands—because it was here that I experienced the reality of God's presence, His faithfulness, and learned the importance of forgiving the Japanese.

"I started fighting in the war in the jungles of Guadalcanal and the Northern Solomon Islands. But nothing that happened there could compare with what I encountered and endured in this your very province. Pointing with my finger, I said, 'I was the first man out that walked that road you can see out the window.'

"The battle at Lupao, just a few kilometers from here, and the vicious fighting in the Caraballo mountains for Balete Pass (renamed Dalton Pass) would test me to the limit. I would know what it meant to be the only target of enemy fire, and experience the terror of hand-to-hand combat.

"On February 28, 1945, on a hill near Maringalo, Nueva Ecija—about three kilometers west of Digdig—our company of soldiers (down to about 150 men) was to occupy a small hill that was shaped like a pear. I was a member of a squad of six strategically placed at the narrow end of the 'pear.' The rest of the company dug their foxholes around the larger and higher ground. Our foxholes, which resembled shallow graves, were

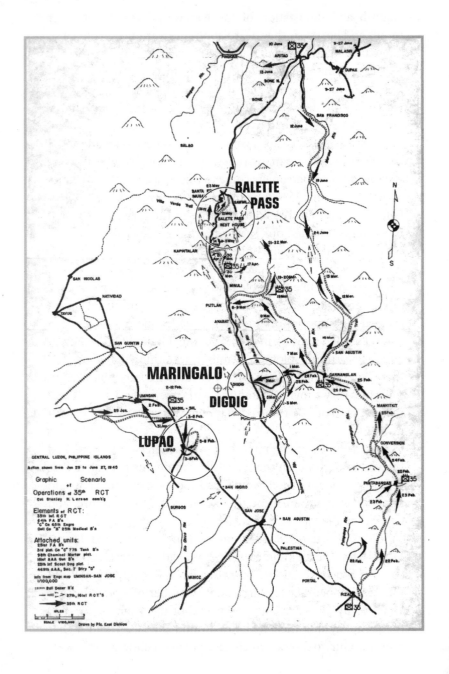

about three feet wide, six feet long and about two feet deep. In these foxholes we lived, and tried to survive every night.

"It was late in the afternoon, when our six-man squad dug in "V" formation. The apex faced outward, in order to protect the sloping ground that was in front of us—three men on one side and three on the other. My hole was near the point of the "V."

"Little did we know that a large detachment of the enemy was about 130 meters away. Under a bush on a little knoll was an observation point from which a person in a prone position could watch our every move. (We learned this a day later, when we captured the knoll.)

"It was about 1:30 A.M. The night had been clear, but now a thick layer of clouds covered the sky. The light of the moon had disappeared. I was awake on guard duty on my side of the "V." In low tones the man who was on duty on the other side and I talked briefly. Everything seemed to be OK. Little did I realize that in a matter of minutes that man would be dead.

"To keep myself alert, I worked on memorizing Bible verses and whole chapters during the night watches. On this very night I was working on Psalm 91, and reviewing Matthew chapters 5, 6, and 7—the Sermon on the Mount. With the light of the moon gone, I stood up, stretched, and then sat down on the edge of my hole. Peace and quietness ruled the evening.

"Suddenly I heard a scuffle, then frightening screams and shouts that pierced the night air from the three members of our squad who were on the other side, about five yards away. There was the clashing of steel as bayonets, rifles, and helmets smashed together. There wasn't time for the men to point their rifles and fire. They were fighting with their fists and anything that they could get their hands on. Sickening cries of anguish and agony filled the darkness. I could hear the strange and eerie sounds of the dying coming from Americans and Japanese alike.

"It was a well-planned attack. The enemy had used the night darkness to try to destroy us. They had chosen to attack at what they thought was the most vulnerable, and yet most strategic point. Soon they were occupying the holes of my comrades. There were thuds, as bodies of my comrades were thrown out of their holes. I looked, and saw only darkness.

"Then against the skyline I caught a glimpse of a raised bayonet ready to strike. I concentrated my rifle fire on the lone figure. It disappeared. I swung my rifle around and began spraying the five-yard space that stood between my side and my three comrades.

"Instinct told me that my comrades were dead, and that it was important to hold our position at any cost. I cried out to the Lord for help—to clear my mind and settle my nerves.

"Now the enemy focused its attack on the three of us on my side. In minutes my sergeant was wounded, and crawled back to the safety of the main body of our troops, on the higher ground behind us.

"The enemy now began to throw grenades at the two of us who were left. I could hear the fuses sizzle as the grenades rolled by, only inches away. It would be only a matter of time before they would hit our holes.

"I crouched. I quickly discussed a strategy with my remaining companion. We should crouch, and if a grenade rolled into our hole, quickly roll out onto the edge, and let the grenade go off. Then roll back into the hole. Japanese grenades had only a three-second fuse, so time was of the essence. We would try to count the seconds. (The fuse on the enemy grenade was started by hitting the activating cap on something hard—a helmet, rifle or stone.)

"As we heard the next 'pop' we started counting. Then it happened—a grenade fell into my comrade's hole, and exploded on his back. I called to him, but there was no answer. The blinding dust from the exploding grenade engulfed us.

"There wasn't time to even try and see if my partner, Jake, was alive. So I continued firing at the enemy. A short time later, I heard a groan, and I shouted for a medic. One brave man crawled out on his stomach, and pulled Jake to the safety of the perimeter and higher ground.

"The situation now was too dangerous for any movement of personnel. The whole American line was awake and tense in the darkness. I could hear the Japanese talking—when there were no shouts from our own men, and there was a break in the din of exploding shells, the chatter of machine guns, and rifle fire.

"My thoughts were racing—*Did the Japanese know that I was alone? Would they rush at me?* If they did, it would be all over. In the terror of the moment I cried out to the Lord for help—especially to calm my pounding heart. There was instant peace, knowing that whether I lived or died I belonged to the Lord.

"The Lord gave me a thought—I had one last option. I shouted for support: 'Give me mortar fire!' (A mortar is fired almost vertically. It goes up in the air about a hundred meters and then comes straight down. It is very effective in tight situations.) My only hope was for the mortar men to pull the shells in so close that they would explode in the five-yard area that was between myself and the enemy on the other side. I was counting on the exploding mortar shells to keep the enemy at bay.

"The mortar shells were coming in dangerously close. Every explosion created clouds of thick dust and smoke that made it difficult to breathe. I waited until I could hear the whistle of the falling shells, then I ducked into the shelter of my hole as the explosion covered me with dirt. After every explosion, I came up firing my rifle.

"I prayed that God would enable me to hang on until daybreak. I knew that daylight would be my salvation. About an hour later, another soldier joined me with a bag of grenades. Three hours later streaks of light filled the sky. Morning was here. I was still alive, but my ammunition was almost gone.

"The Japanese were now talking excitedly, and there was movement. They were grunting and struggling, as they prepared to retreat with their dead and wounded. They disappeared in the early morning shadows.

"Daylight exposed the carnage. Two of my buddies were dead, their bodies scattered among the corpses of the enemy. A third comrade, whose hole was with the men who died, had his right hand almost severed when he grabbed a Japanese bayonet by the blade and kept it from being thrust into his heart.

"He told me: 'He was there on top of me, and then suddenly he was gone.' As I reflected on the evening, I remembered seeing one shadowy figure with a raised rifle and fixed bayonet. It was the only visible sign of anyone I had seen all night long!

"After crouching for over three hours, my cramped legs could hardly lift me to a standing position. I looked in my own foxhole, and there on the floor were two mortar fins. They reminded me of how close death had come.

"The captain congratulated me: 'You single-handedly saved the company by holding your ground. I am putting you in for a medal.'

"For me the whole event was a miracle! God had spared my life.

"About a month later I received letters from my father in Oakland, California and my brother in Wheaton, Illinois. By Asian time reckoning, both had an urge to pray for me. My father asked his boss to excuse him so that he could pray for his son. And my brother left his college classroom to pray. The timing was exactly right. The two were simultaneously praying for me as I was under fire.

"The captain was mistaken! I was not alone, and I did not do it single-handedly. God was with me. Later on when the Philippines was secured and we were pulled off the lines, I was decorated with the Silver Star medal by our commanding general. The citation read in part '...for gallantry in action against the enemy ... bravery ... courage.'

"The men congratulated me as a 'hero,' but I didn't feel that way. I had done what every soldier was expected to do. For me personally it was an opportunity to witness to the members of my company, telling them that there is a God, and that He was taking care of me. This was one crowning point of many

The author on the day he was decorated with the Silver Star by
Major General Mullins, Commanding Officer of the 25th Division,
Camp Patrick, near Clark Air Base, Philippines, on June 25, 1945.

situations, where it had been my heavenly Father looking after me. One comrade close to me said, 'You are more like a cat with nine lives than a human!'

"Friends, other events took place to confirm the validity of my negative feelings towards the enemy. I had every reason to be angry at the enemy, and bitter and unforgiving. Actually I have thirty-two reasons to be unforgiving—that is the number of men who had died out of my original company that had landed on this island.

"The cruelty of the Japanese and their vicious retaliation against captured Filipinos and Americans made my blood boil with rage. The enemy seemed to delight in extreme torture.

"The one most excruciating pain, which was reserved for Americans, was the water treatment. The enemy would put a hose into the mouth, fill the stomach with water and then take turns jumping on the victim's stomach! Death came very slowly.

"The Philippine guerrillas, who were continually joining us, gave accounts of executions and unexpected violent actions. We met one band of men who hid from the Japanese during the whole occupation. They fought the enemy with bare hands, clubs, and wire.

"Their leader, who became one of our scouts, said that he had been a farmer in the mountains until a Japanese patrol entered his village. They questioned him, but were dissatisfied with his answers. Without warning, a Japanese officer smashed him in the face with the butt of his rifle. All his front teeth were knocked out, and his jaw was broken. They left him for dead.

"From that moment on, the man became a Japanese hunter, looking for enemy stragglers. He had a wire about one meter long, which was tied to two short sticks at each end. He would sneak up behind a straggler, loop the wire over the unsuspecting victim's head, and with a jerk pull the wire. It was so quick, so sudden a decapitation, that a person would be gone without a sound. He demonstrated, wrapping his wire around a young coconut tree that was approximately the size of a human neck, and pulled. He made believers out of us all. He also proved to be a fearless and valuable partner in tracking the enemy. It was a pleasure to have him on our side.

"I didn't sleep well last night, but I was thinking beyond the war and the enemy. My thoughts were focused on you here, who have never forgiven the Japanese.

"The sights and sounds of the war on that particular night in Maringalo, and other nights and days similar to that one, have never left me. But when these things come back to haunt me, there is an escape. I learned from Matthew 6:14,15: 'For if you forgive men when they sin against you, your heavenly Father will also forgive you. But if you do not forgive men their sins, your Father will not forgive your sins.' By forgiving others—including the Japanese—there is forgiveness for us."

Then I challenged the pastors to forgive not only the Japanese as a people, but the Japanese as the enemy, so together we could be free. There was a tremendous response, with men asking the Lord for forgiveness and committing themselves to Him.

It was now time for lunch, and I hastened to pass through the cafeteria line. A pastor without a lunch tray sat down across from me. There was concern on his face. He said that he wanted to talk with me about my message.

He said, "Thank you for sharing to us all about the war, and the Japanese. Everything you said is true." There was a long and nervous hesitation; then his next words caught me off guard: "I am married to a Japanese."

Now I was flustered, nervous, and speechless. When finally I could talk, I said, "Please forgive me, if I have in any way offended you or your wife."

"Oh no!" he said. "It was all right. My wife knows about the cruelty of her own people. It has been an embarrassment to her for a long time. She grieves over the conduct of the Japanese occupation soldiers. But it is difficult for her to say anything about it. She simply remains silent, when it comes to talking about the war."

My curiosity now had the best of me. I had to ask, "How in the world did you two get together?"

He then told me that his wife came to the Philippines in response to her mother's desire that she serve the Lord in the most dangerous place in the world for the Japanese—the Philippines! The Lord had spared her mother's life during the American bombing raids on Japan. In thankfulness to the Lord for this, she wanted her daughter to become a missionary.

By now other pastors had joined us, and my newfound friend became silent. After lunch he said he knew his wife would want to meet me sometime. He invited me to come to his church in the future to speak in a Sunday morning service, and above all else to meet his wife.

At this time it was not my intent to travel the five-hour trip to Central Luzon again. The roads were treacherous, and the danger from communist insurgency discouraged me from even thinking about it. But the conversation at lunch break with this pastor regarding his wife haunted me. One night in Manila, when sleep had left me, the Lord turned my thoughts to Nueva Ecija, and this woman. I knew in my heart that before I left the Philippines I would have to meet her.

28

JAPANESE MISSIONARY IN THE PHILIPPINES

SEPTEMBER 1990

I t was the second week of September. In order to avoid the daily traffic crunch in Manila I was up at 3:00 A.M., and on my way back to Nueva Ecija province. I had a very uneasy feeling. As I journeyed north I was very apprehensive about meeting the Japanese wife of the Filipino pastor whom I had met at the conference three months earlier.

He had asked me to share in the Sunday morning service on "The Challenge of Missions" for which I was well prepared. But the events of the morning would force me to make a radical change in my sermon plan.

I arrived at 8:00 A.M. and Sunday School was in session. The pastor greeted me warmly, and said that his wife, Phoebe, would like to meet with me privately in their home, which was right next door to the church.

I was ushered into the presence of a woman with a beautiful smile. The joy on her face melted away my anxiety. It was necessary to look at her face very carefully so as to distinguish her from a Filipina. Her manners and graciousness exemplified the best from both cultures. She shook my hand with feeling, and I knew that she wanted to be my friend.

She closed the door, and we were alone. She told me that her husband had shared everything that I had said at the conference about the Japanese. She was so ashamed because of what her people had done in the Philippines during the occupation. She went on to say that she had always wanted to be able to completely express her feelings, but could never quite do it.

Now I had to ask a question before we talked about anything else: "What is it in your background that brought you from Japan to this country?" She smiled and gave me this exciting account.

"My mother's family lived in a village that was near Tokyo, and they were subject to constant air raids from U.S. airplanes. When the planes came, my mother would run to a nearby park where there was an air raid shelter.

"As the war approached a climax, the air raids became more intensive, and there was talk of an invasion by U.S. forces. All the women were being trained how to fight off the Americans. They were told that the soldiers were coming to rape, and to kill.

"By now there was little metal left in the country for knives or bullets to defend themselves. Our own soldiers stripped every piece of metal from every home—hinges from the doors of my mother's house, and even my mother's rings were taken from her fingers. Their weapon against the invading soldiers would be bamboo—fashioned into knives with a razor edge.

"I was born about two months before the war ended. Just days before the surrender, the U.S. forces unleashed an incendiary raid, which set my mother's village on fire. She had me tied on her back, and as before, she ran for cover. On the way the ashes were so thick that they covered me. When my mother unstrapped me and looked, she found a thick layer of ashes over my face. She thought I was dead! But God had spared my life.

"It was late autumn when the U.S. forces arrived, and the whole country was terrified. But instead of rape and killings, the soldiers treated everyone with kindness. The U.S. soldiers put away their rifles and roamed the villages, giving out blankets, food, and candy. My mother and the villagers were bewildered by this!

"Because of the kindness of the American soldiers, the people in my mother's village gathered together to discuss this strange but wonderful enemy! They agreed on one thing. These soldiers from America are supposed to represent the Christian religion. If this is the way Christians act, then we will accept their God as our God. My mother, along with about 100 others in her village gave their hearts to the Americans' God—later they learned about the Bible and Jesus Christ.

"My mother was a Christian from that day forward. When I grew older, she urged me to become a Christian. I was rebellious at first, but finally gave my heart to Jesus. It was a short time later that my mother challenged me.

"She said that as an act of thanksgiving, I should serve the living and the true God by becoming a missionary. But that wasn't all. 'You must go to the most dangerous place on earth for a Japanese!' she said. That was here!

"When I first came, I fully believed that I would be martyred. But the Lord had spared my life, and now this people has become my people."

What a testimony of forgiveness! I realized that my so-called "sacrifice" to come back to this country as a missionary was insignificant compared to what she had done.

Being in her presence went by quickly. Now it was time for the morning worship service. She told me that she would be playing the organ and praying for me, as she eagerly waited to hear my message. She bowed, then slipped away quickly.

In many Filipino churches it is the custom that the choir and the pastor march down the aisle to the platform during the first hymn. This would be the procedure for this service. I looked to the front of the church and could see Phoebe, seated at the organ, facing toward the pulpit on the right. On the other side of the platform was the pianist, facing the pulpit on the left.

Suddenly Phoebe got up from the organ and came back to me. I could see by her countenance that she was agitated. She grabbed my hand and said, "Pastor, please tell the congregation exactly what you shared at the conference. I want the people to hear everything."

I answered, "But Phoebe, I am here to speak on missions, not to talk about the war. I am not prepared. Besides, the war happened so long ago."

She would not let go of my hand or take no for an answer. I was confused. Now the music from the piano signaled that it was time to march down the aisle. I was in battle again! All I could do was cry out to the Lord with a big *Help!*

In that moment the Lord gave me peace regarding her request, so I said, "Yes, I'll do it." She gave me a smile of satisfaction and returned to her seat at the organ.

It was a difficult time, as I launched into my sharing, which really wasn't much of a message. I could see Phoebe out of the corner of my eye. Every time I mentioned the Japanese her face turned a brilliant red, and the congregation would switch its focus from me to her, and would laugh. She didn't look to the right or the left, but kept her face fixed on me.

I learned early on that the Filipino laughter is a cultural way of expressing a feeling of embarrassment, but this merely added to my tension during the service. There was no question about it—this was very humiliating for her, and unsettling for me. I had to do something.

The Lord turned on the light! The ugliness of the morning turned to beauty as I called for a time of heart-searching and forgiveness. In part, I said, "There are many of you older people here who remember the war, but have never forgiven the Japanese. Now is the time to get things right with the Japanese and the Lord." The response was overwhelming, and I knew that the Lord had done a great work.

When the service was over, Phoebe asked to talk with me

in private once more. I agreed, and we retired to her home. She grasped my hand, and said, "I can't say thank-you enough for what you shared. This is something that I wanted to do ever since I came here eighteen years ago. Now I am free, because of what you shared. Thank you. Today the burden of my heart has been lifted."

After lunch with her family, I was on my way home with a new appreciation of the impact of the war. Even after forty-five years, God was still doing exciting things in my heart and in the hearts of the Filipinos!

EPILOGUE

I n God's grand plan He meant the war for good! This sounds almost cruel. However, in looking back in history on more than one occasion, God has turned ashes into beauty.

I am reminded of Joseph's testimony to his brothers, when he referred back to his horrible experience of being sold into slavery: "Don't be afraid. Am I in the place of God? You intended to harm me, but God intended it for good to accomplish what is now being done, the saving of many lives" (Genesis 50:19,20).

In the book of Jeremiah 29:11-14 it states strongly that God's plans for us are for good and not for evil, although the discipline we endure may be long and severe.

In reflecting back on the twentieth century I can see God's hand at work. To some the past seems like a curse, but to others those years have become a blessing. What seemed like humiliation and defeat for the Philippines turned out to be a blessing in disguise.

The turn of the past century brought the Spanish-American War. The Filipinos wanted freedom from Spain, and Jose Rizal, their national hero, gave his life for the cause. Then they struggled against the Americans for independence. But their plan of a free country was not to be. They got rid of the Spanish, but they ended up being under the control of the United States of America.

This conquest brought a military governor by the name of Gen. Arthur MacArthur (father of Gen. Douglas MacArthur).

One of his decrees would set the Philippine nation on a track of blessing that would have worldwide significance.

He had two major tasks: First, to unite this nation of islands. The second was even more formidable—to communicate with a country that had over eighty languages and dialects.[1]

Early in the 1900s he declared that only English should be spoken in the schools. But he needed help. So he made an appeal to teachers in the United States to come, and join him in the task. The response was amazing. Over 2,300 teachers, many of whom were Christians, accepted the call that enabled him to achieve both objectives—unity and communication.

During the early '50s, in my first tour of duty in the Philippines as a missionary, I had the privilege of meeting some of these teachers, who had now reached retirement age. This land of beautiful islands and smiling people was now their adopted home. They had chosen to stay in the Philippines, and not to return to America. Their lasting legacy is that they taught English to the Filipino people.

In 1998 I had a chance meeting with a woman whose grandparents, the Pruitts (real name), were a part of that "team of teachers" who came to the Philippines. When she heard that I had been a liberation soldier, we bonded immediately. She went to her bookshelf and brought out pictures of her grandparents, standing with beaming Filipino children. In glowing terms, she shared a number of stories of her grandparents' experiences. She recalled their years of service with great love, joy, and affection.

Then World War II came, with Gen. Douglas MacArthur's famous statement, "I shall return." He kept his promise but did not return alone. He came back with over 150,000 soldiers. They all became "teachers" in their own unique ways, and English reached a new level of impact throughout the nation. Today it is spoken by almost everyone in the Philippines.

Little did any of us know that this gift of English would lay the foundation for Filipinos to become effective missionaries in the world. Today English serves as their "bridge language" in learning many difficult languages. English must be understood first before a missionary can start learning any of the many languages of other countries.

There are now over 2,000 Filipino missionaries scattered all over the globe. Having been equipped with the English language, they are enabled to effectively communicate the Gospel in a language of their host countries. And this is just the beginning. There are many more Filipinos in training, who have set their sights on reaching other nations with the Gospel.

It was in God's grand plan that the two wars would turn the Philippines into a critical missionary force. In that grand plan there was a small part that I should play.

In 1945 God brought me to the Philippines with Gen. Douglas MacArthur as a foot soldier. It was not my plan in the beginning. But God directed my steps, and Proverbs 16:9 became a reality: "In his heart a man plans his course, but the Lord determines his steps."

In 1953 God directed my steps, along with my wife's, to serve as missionaries in the Philippines, and we have been involved with this land and people ever since.

The Protestant Church in the Philippines celebrated its centennial in 1998. It has been an honor and privilege to have contributed in a small part to the spiritual growth of this great nation, and to have been a part of its history for greater than half of a century.

This country has become my country, and its people my people! And the Japanese? They have become my special friends.

NOTES

CHAPTER 1

1. Guadalcanal is the biggest of the Solomon Islands in Melanesia. It was the first of the series of islands retaken by the United States from Japan marking the end of the Japanese territorial gains. In the six-month struggle for this "Island of Death,"(the longest in the entire Pacific war) Americans got their first taste of jungle warfare. *(Illustrated Story of World War II,* NY: Readers' Digest Asia Limited, 1970, p.215). The Solomon Islands is an archipelago in the West Pacific Ocean, east of New Guinea *(Random House Unabridged Dictionary,* 2nd ed., 1993).

2. New Caledonia is an island in the South Pacific about eight hundred miles east of Australia *(Random House...)*

3. At this time the Philippines was a U.S. colony having been ceded by Spain to the United States upon the signing of the Treaty of Paris in December 1898, and its ratification by the U.S. Congress on February 6, 1899. In Asia the Philippines was among the first countries to be attacked by Japan after the bombing of Pearl Harbor.

4. Gen. MacArthur's plan was to drive the enemy away from fortified positions both in and around Manila and fight them in the Central Luzon plain.

CHAPTER 2

1. Dr. Met "Mr. Missions" Castillo is founder of Great Commission Missionary Training. He joined Overseas Crusade (OC) (now OC International, Inc.) in 1982.

CHAPTER 3

1. Refrain of an old favorite, "Turn Your Eyes Upon Jesus," lyrics and music by Helen Howarth Lemmel.

CHAPTER 4

1. Rosario, a place just below Pozorrubio on the map, not Rosario, La Union.

CHAPTER 20

1. *Illustrated Story of World War II* has 3,000 only. But Louis Morton, the official U.S. military historian, states that there were 78,000 men under Maj. Gen.

Edward P. King in Bataan, and only 2,000 were able to escape to Corregidor including 300 survivors of the 31st Infantry (US) (L. Morton, *The Fall of the Philippines*, Washington, DC: *1953*, p. 461). Stanley L. Falk, Morton's research assistant, records that there were 78,100 men (66,304 Filipinos and 11,796 Americans) in Bataan. Of these, 4,200 Filipino soldiers did not join the Death March: 2,500 remained in the hospitals in Bataan, and 1,700 escaped to Corregidor. Among the Americans, 1,875 did not join the Death March: 1,500 stayed in the hospitals, 300 escaped to Corregidor, 25 remained to do work for the Japanese, and 50 simply escaped. Excluded here is the statistic for Corregidor which is 13,193 men rounded up as POW in barb wire enclosure (Antonio Varias, *A Compilation on World War II in the Philippines*, 1970, p.123). Col. Marshall recorded 44,000 Filipino soldiers to have arrived in prison (Capas) (Gen. Lawrence and Col. Glatty gave slightly higher figures). Of the Americans, 9,921 reached Camp O'donell in Nueva Ecija which was converted into a prison camp. An estimate of 5,000 to 10,000 Filipinos and 650 Americans died along the way. Inside the POW camps, 1,600 Americans and 29,180 Filipino soldiers died (P. Catalan and E. Calderon, *A Brief History of the 51st Division*, p.183 cited in C. Quirino, *Filipinos at War*, Vera-Reyes, Inc., 1981, p.225.)

CHAPTER 23

1. *Konichiwa* is used as a greeting after 10:00 A.M.

EPILOGUE

1. The latest counts from the Summer Institute of Linguistics are 110 languages (Curtis McFarland, "Subgrouping and Number of Philippine Languages [or How many Philippine languages are there?]," *Philippine Journal of Linguistics*, v.25, nos. 1 & 2, 1994) and 171 major languages (*Ethnologue: Languages of the world*, 13th ed., 1996).

GLOSSARY

artillery/mortar—Long and short range cannons for support of the infantry.

banzai attack—Suicide attack usually by a group of Japanese soldiers.

bunker—Shelter underground used by soldiers.

bunker slit—A narrow opening through which a soldier can observe or fire at the enemy.

charge—Amount of explosive needed to cause an explosion.

GI, GI Joe, or Doughboy—Common names given to any American soldier. (GI stands for Government Issue.)

infantry—Branch of an army composed of units trained to fight on foot.

kamikaze—Japanese pilots or soldiers trained to make suicidal attacks.

maringalo—*(Maringalu)* A barrio or village situated just to the right of Digdig. (Digdig is along the national highway about halfway between San Jose, Nueva Ecija and Sta. Fe, Nueva Vizcaya.)

occupation scrip—Worthless money that the Japanese issued in the Philippines.

perimeter (of defense)—A circle or a line of men behind which there are friendly forces.

sapper—Soldier carrying out engineering work, e.g., roads and bridges; they use dynamite.

(Refer to next page regarding squad, platoon, company, battalion, regiment and division.)

COMPONENTS OF AN ARMY (1942-45)

UNIT	RANK OF COMMANDING OFFICER	COMPOSITION AND NUMBER OF MEN	EXAMPLE
Division (includes attached units e.g., Engineers, Field Artillery, Tanks)	Major General (Maj. Gen.)	3 regiments (15,000 men)	25th Division 21st Division 5th Division etc.
Regiment	Colonel (Col.)	3 battalions (3,000 men)	27th Infantry 35th Infantry 161st Infantry
Battalion	Lieutenant Colonel (Lt. Col.) or Major (Maj.)	4 companies (1,000 men)	1st Battalion 2nd Battalion
Company	Captain (Capt.)	4 platoons (200 men)	"L" Company "I" Company
Platoon	Lieutenant (Lieut.)	4 squads (42 men)	2nd Platoon 4th Platoon
Squad	Staff or Buck Sergeant (Sgt.) (non-comissioned officer)	10-12 men	1st Squad

NON-COMMISSIONED OFFICERS*

First Sergeant	Top Noncom in the company
Sergeant First Class**	Top Noncom in the platoon
Staff Sergeant	Squad Leader (sometimes top man in the platoon)
Buck Sergeant	Asst Squad Leader (at times squad leader)
Corporal	Asst Squad Leader (under certain conditions)
Private First Class (any private with good conduct)	Scout or point man (usually would be promoted after 18 months of active duty)
Private	Regular foot soldier (could be a scout or point man)

* The responsibilities of the Noncom during the war.
** My rank when I ended my army career.

WORK IN THE KINGDOM

CHARLES D. HOLSINGER
TOUR OF DUTY

6th Army under Gen. Walter Krueger

25th Division

35th Infantry Regiment

3rd Battalion

"K" Company

1st Platoon

1st Squad

1924 Mar 8	Born in Red Bluff, CA; father was a pastor; both parents planned to be in missions; Mother's health changed their plans
1930 Spring	I asked Jesus to come into my life
1942 Fall	Went off to Wheaton College
1942 Dec 12	Called to active duty in the Army and trained as a front-line soldier
1943 Jul 7	Sailed out from San Francisco Bay for an unknown destination in the Pacific
1943 Aug	Arrived in Guadalcanal Island and assigned to the 25th Division; first contact with the enemy
1943 Sep	First invasion experience, Vella LaVella island; little fighting, but heavy air raids daily
1943 Oct	First observation of missionary work in Vella LaVella; impacted me profoundly
1943 Dec	25th Division taken to New Zealand for rest and recreation
1944 Mar	25th Division assigned to New Caledonia Island for retraining and preparation for an invasion
1945 Jan	We invade Luzon, Philipines

1945 Aug	Japan Surrenders
1945 Nov	Member, Occupation Force, Japan
1945 Dec	Return to USA
1949 Jun	Graduated from Wheaton College, Wheaton, Ill, BA Degree
1949 Aug	Married Elisabeth Hermansen
1949-53	Assistant football coach at Wheaton and youth worker
1953	Master's Degree from Wheaton College
1953 Sept	Sailed for Philippines
1955-56	Stateside with hepatitis
1957-74	Coach, teacher, administrator at school for missionary and US military children, Morrison Academy, Taichung, Taiwan
1974 Sep	Appointed Director, Home Ministries, OC International
1980 Jun	Appointed Director of Sports Ambassadors (formerly known in the Philippines as Venture for Victory.)
1980 Dec	Appointed Vice-President, OC International
1982 Mar	Sent to meet and interview Dr. Met Castillo to join OC
1984 Jun	Appointed Administrative Director, China Radio Ministry
1985	Appointed Executive Vice-President, OC International; to travel worldwide to counsel missionaries
1986	Sent to Philippines as Pastors' Conference speaker
1989	Assigned to Philippines as Assistant Field Director (to free Dr. Met Castillo to devote full time to Asian Mission Congress)
1990 Mar	Took over as Field Director, Philippines: involved in seminars, pastors' sharing war experiences. Subsequently appointed Asst. Area Director, Asia
1990 Sep	Awarded honorary doctor's degree by Harvest Bible Seminary, Cabanatuan City, Philippines
1991 Jan	Moved to Manila to direct the field; involved in church planting seminars
1992 Jul	Appointed Area Director, Europe
1997 Jan	Appointed Asst. Area Director, Latin America and Asst. Director, International Ministry Team
1998 Jan	Appointed Asst. to Vice-President, Fields
1999 Mar	Celebrated as a couple forty-six years of ministry with OC International
1999 Nov 28	Celebrated the opening of the new Great Commission Missionary Training Center, Antipolo, Rizal, Philippines

APPENDIX

HEADQUARTERS 25th INFANTRY DIVISION
Office of the Commanding General

GENERAL ORDERS   A.P.O. *25*
NUMBER 276   *25* June 1945

AWARD OF THE SILVER STAR

By direction of the President, under the provision of the act of Congress approved 9 July 1918, (Bul 43,WD, 1918), a Silver Star is awarded by the Commanding General, 25th Infantry Division, to the following named enlisted man:

Private First Class Charles D. Holsinger,
16170833, Infantry, United States Army

For gallantry in action against the Japanese forces at Maringalu*, Luzon, Philippine Islands on 28 February 1945. During a night attack upon his company position, the enemy infiltrated into the six-man strong point of which Private First Class HOLSINGER was a member. After killing two men, wounding one and forcing one to withdraw, the enemy occupied the four positions to his left and concentrated rifle fire and grenades upon him. Although he was now alone, with no thought of retreat he coolly returned fire and directed assault mortar fire on the enemy not more than five yards from his position. He held his position for one hour until joined by another soldier carrying hand grenades. At dawn he assisted in clearing the enemy from the positions they had taken.

Private First Class HOLSINGER'S gallant actions in the face of grave danger, which limited the enemy's infiltration and enabled his platoon to hold its ground, were in keeping with the highest traditions of the military service.

Home Address: Mr. Paul H. Holsinger, Father,
Route 9, Box 1860, Sacramento, California.

BY COMMAND OF MAJOR GENERAL MULLINS

*Army spelling; Philipino spelling is Maringalo.

Above the Cry of Battle
Order Form

Postal orders: Chuck Holsinger
399 W. Overlook Dr.
Upland, IN 46989

Telephone orders: 765-998-7709

E-mail orders: cdhbpsinet.com

Please send *Above the Cry of Battle* **to:**

Name: _____

Address: _____

City: _____ State: _____

Zip: _____

Telephone: (_____) _____

Book Price: $13.00

Shipping: $3.00 for the first book and $1.00 for each additional book to
cover shipping and handling within US, Canada, and Mexico.
International orders add $6.00 for the first book and $2.00 for
each additional book.

Or order from:
ACW Press
5501 N. 7th. Ave. #502
Phoenix, AZ 85013

(800) 931-BOOK

or contact your local bookstore